*The*
# TRANSIENT

For Dave

and

(as he would have made sure was included)

For any creature who has lost another

*The*

# TRANSIENT

## A Memoir and Meditations on the Loss of a Younger Sibling

### Judy Evans, MD

MCP - Maitland, FL

Mill City Press, Inc.
2301 Lucien Way #415
Maitland, FL 32751
407·339·4217
www.millcitypublishing.com

ISBN-13: 978-1-63505-475-0

Acknowledgment: very special thanks to my dad and mom, unfailingly supportive in every way

Cover image: The Transient, oil on canvas (Judy Evans). Based on an image from a video short piece entitled "Graffiti: An Urban Art," a Static Euphoria production created and directed by Joshua D. Schray and featured in 2004 at the South Side Film Festival (Bethlehem, PA), the Moravian College Student Film Festival (Bethlehem, PA), and the Square Dance Film Festival (Northampton, PA), where it was shown at the historic landmark Roxy Theater.

*Printed in the United States of America*

# CONTENTS

## III. Discovery

## IV. Treasure

## V. THE LONGING AFTER: ENSUING YEARS

# Prologue

An ordinary Friday night: no work tomorrow, so I've gotten home late from a dance party. I've stayed up even later reading a novel, and after 3 a.m. I finally go to bed, suspecting nothing.

Miles away in the middle of the night, a random car has become a statistic. It has swerved, slipped, tumbled, and smashed on the side of a road, but this has nothing to do with me. Not until hours later, when I'm on the phone listening to my dad describe the car and what happened to it. Riding in this car were my twenty-two-year-old little brother Dave, and two of his friends. The facts are quick: one car; three people; two survivors. I'm blank, perplexed, which leaves my dad no choice. He has to name the one who died.

A film plays in my head, but it's not what I imagine has happened to my little brother. It's not something I imagine at all. It merely appears, and the person in the film is me:

*Living. Out of nowhere, struck from behind, flung forward . . . falling . . . going down. I'm both the one it's happening to and the one who watches: falling, out of control, crashing down. There is no knowledge of what's happening, only a sense that things are coming apart that shouldn't. At last the face I know as my own comes to rest against the ground. The neck may or may not be broken. If there is still breath, it's impossible to tell.*

*The eyes are open, but there is no amazement, no awareness—only an idea that a moment ago, the person I know as "I" had simply been living, but just now, that person has gone down. It's myself I'm watching, but I'm not aware of anything except that something elemental has changed.*

**\* \* \***

    The concept is simple, requiring only a handful of words— *your*, *little*, *sibling*, *is*, and *dead*—yet when you learn of it, there is no true comprehension. There is only a sense that a moment ago you had simply been living, but just now, you've been cut down. Things are coming apart that shouldn't. Whether you're still breathing, it's impossible to tell. And something elemental has most certainly changed.

**LOSS**

## Chapter 1

# Rosa

(Wishing)

*R*osa is a book. When I first read the story, I was about six years old. From the time I was very small, I was one of those kids who reads at the dinner table, reads in the car, hovers like a moth at the nightlight in order to sneak-read long past bedtime. My favorites, stories I'd checked out over and over from the library, were mostly wistful or even sad: *Amy Loves Goodbye*, *The Day After Yesterday*, *May I Visit*...common themes of departure, absence, and lostness were like different melodies from the same symphony, written in a minor key. But *Rosa* was different altogether: it was about pure happiness. Written by Leo Politi and illustrated in festive pinks and greens and blues and browns, the book tells of a Mexican schoolgirl who lives with her family near San Felipe. Accompanied by her older brother José, Rosa goes about her daily life until one day, it's time to make a wish for Christmas. For months, Rosa has been yearning for a doll she has seen in a store window, but she knows her family can't afford such an extravagance. Is there any chance that Rosa, a pleasant and dutiful girl, could ever get the longed-for doll? As it turns out, what she gets exceeds her dreams: on Christmas Eve, her mother gives birth to a baby girl. Rosa is a big sister—there is a *real* baby!

When I first read the story, this outcome seemed to climb out of the book and snuggle up like a contented kitten in my arms.

3

I studied the picture of Rosa and her brother dashing to join their happy parents, the cozy thatched-roof hut aglow in the indigo dusk. At the center of the glow was a white-diapered baby, a tiny gem: that "real baby" was the most irresistible thing I had ever seen. Even then, I'd known such an event wouldn't happen in my own house, of course; my parents already had three children, and life was chaotic enough, so I automatically consigned the idea of a baby sibling to the long list of wishes you don't hope for because you already know they don't come true. Strictly a fantasy.

Like Rosa, I'd been a baby-doll girl, although by the time I was nine I'd begun to outgrow dolls in favor of new interests like a balance beam, rose-pink nail polish, and a bike with a white basket on the front. What happened next, I never saw coming. In the autumn of that year, when my brother Tim was eleven and my brother Mike was eight, my mother announced that she was going to have a baby the following summer. She looked at my prettily painted fingernails and said, "If you want to help with the baby, you have to cut your nails short." I sheared my nails without a second thought. I was prepared to give up nail polish, reading, eating, or sleeping if it meant I could help with the baby.

We older kids were democratically included in the process of selecting a name, and the July day on which my parents brought baby Matthew home from the hospital was a quietly thrilling, picnic kind of day, special enough to merit McDonald's for lunch. The family ranged about on the back porch in the midsummer heat, but my hamburger and fries lay only half-eaten on the old-fashioned metal milk box because I couldn't keep myself away from the living room and the white wicker bassinette gleaming against the far wall. I tiptoed alone into the room and peered reverently into the bassinette to gaze upon the new baby: black-haired and wearing a diaper, he lay curled like a tiny comma against the vastness of cotton sheet. With fearful gentleness I reached down and smoothed his silken head; having already studied my mother's old nursing school textbooks, I knew about infant skulls and their soft spots, the fontanels. The caution had been very clear: the newborn skull is vulnerable; the head should be touched only with great care.

I knew how ridiculously unlikely it was for a storybook fantasy to have come true, but it came true for me not once but twice. Two years later, my mother brought home her fifth and last baby, the wispy-curled youngest whom we'd named David. I received him from my overworked mother's arms, my own twelve-year-old arms already skilled in the ballet of baby-holding: supporting the wobbly neck, you carefully tuck the tiny warm entireness against your shoulder as your arms curve into an arabesque like an upright cradle, and then a walk is a dance is a lullaby, and you rest your cheek against his little knockabout head, which he uses to tell you what he's thinking of, what he wants next, or just that you've made the cradle the right way and he knows your presence so very well.

\* \* \*

A baby who lives with us every day bestows an unguarded trust. Before we might experience such an exquisite thing, we may have to live patiently through countless days, months, maybe many years. Maybe the patience is futile; maybe we'll wait and wish forever, and it will never come to pass. Or maybe it will.

# Chapter 2

# The Bébés

(Wish Fulfillment)

Tim, Mike, and I learned how to make hot rice cereal, how to change cloth diapers, and how to sponge mashed carrots out of a baby's hair. From our dad we learned how the situation is to be managed when a toddler stuffs a raisin up its own nostril. We learned from our mother how to take a little kid swimming in a big pool, and we figured out for ourselves how to balance a baby brother with his stomach on the soles of our upraised stocking feet so he could be a plane in flight, a seagull, or just giddily aloft. How to carry little kids when you're both tired: lift them up behind your neck, plop them on your shoulders, and hang on to their knees to keep them from toppling from their human throne. They can survey the world from on high, and to show their contentment, they grab fistfuls of your hair and drool in it (and if you're lucky, only drool). We obliged with gusto when asked to read Dr. Seuss's *Fox in Sox* for the 837th time; we learned by heart scenes of *Winnie the Pooh* and quotes from *Inspector Gadget*. Bits of dialogue from children's TV shows, books, and songs permeated the family lexicon and remain there to this day.

By the age of two, Matthew was already nearly a master of the English language, and David emerged from his baby-bird infancy with an aureole of wayward light brown curls, an impish smile, and a tendency to observe quietly. Tim, Mike, and I had long since fallen under their spell; if our mother so much as walked past carrying one of the babies, we would lean down to nuzzle them in passing, sniffing their heads gently like a bunch of besotted giraffes. And we were flat-out ridiculous about pet names and endearments. When our parents bought a baby seat designed to be attached to a bicycle, we older kids spotted the French words on the packaging calling it a *porte-bébé*. Immediately, Matt and Dave became "the bébés," and over time, they would answer to any of a hundred different nicknames, from Bébé to Porta, from Pumpkin to Pooka-tooka-shnookins.

We grew up, and so did the bébés. We went to high school, they went to elementary school…we went away to college, and they grew into their own adolescence…we finished college, they graduated high school. Our lives diverged and converged like meandering tributaries, the passing years marked by the innumerable milestones of childhood. Each year, the "Happy Birthday" sign my mother hung up in March stayed there until September because everyone's birthday fell within that stretch of exactly six months; no sooner would one person's birthday pass than it was time to prepare for someone else's, so it simply made sense to leave the sign up for the entire summer.

Long after Dave had grown more than a foot taller than me, every now and then I'd look at him and crow "Little Shnooks!" for no reason. He always smiled, graciously allowing me this minor indulgence without protest. Perhaps he saw it as harmless, just silly-silliness. Maybe he was cringing inside with embarrassment that I could be that much of a dork, or possibly he secretly basked because he'd figured out the real translation.

\* \* \*

It's a natural sort of nostalgia, to "miss" someone who's sitting right there. We're not trying to infantilize them; we're just recalling the younger version of them and maybe recalling the younger version of ourselves, too. Sometimes, we hesitate. Embarrassment yanks the reins on our unbroken affection, keeps us from articulating what we might think is too foolish, so instead we blurt out silly nicknames that somehow contain all that we can't say.

The real translation: *It is amazing that you are so tall and old and accomplished, yet sometimes your very maturity itself limns the memory of a baby whose sheer lovability was an outrage against the laws of nature— adorable beyond words, adorable in a way only nonsense and cuckoo pet names could begin to manage. Somehow you are who you are now, and also who you were then, at the same time...and in the bittersweet incongruity I get momentarily confused and call you Little Shnooks again, accidentally on purpose...maybe just to tell you: you're as perfectly you now, as you were then. Or maybe just to tell you: I remember.*

## Chapter 3

# May-Day

### (*That* Day)

On the final night of April 2004, I've been at a Friday party at the ballroom dance studio where I take lessons. Typically such parties tire me out, and by way of refreshment afterward, I sit down at the kitchen table in my solitary apartment and submerge my mind in the hot bath of a book. The trick is to stay up as long as possible, to make sure that I don't "go" to bed but instead stumble there blindly, drugged with tiredness and therefore safe from insomnia.

Tonight, the book I'm reading is a novel called *The Secret History*, by Diana Tartt. For hours I'm absorbed in this story about a group of academically elite students who unwittingly lose themselves in a moral nightmare of their own making. I keep reading until it gets difficult to reopen my eyes after each blink, but still I drag my gaze through another chapter, and another, knowing I'm being absurd but unable to stop. By three-thirty a.m., I could literally close my eyes and lose consciousness sitting at the table. Instead I put the book facedown on the table, turn out the kitchen light, and tread numbly upstairs to bed.

At an unknown time, from underneath a blanket of oblivion, I hear my old-fashioned pager buzzing and the telephone ringing in the distance. The answering machine downstairs picks up, but I can't hear the messages that are being left on it. I'm sedated with

11

fatigue and sink back into unconsciousness, until finally, around ten o'clock in the morning, I crawl out of bed. It's the first of May. I look at my pager and see the calls, all from my parents' home number. Puzzled, I call them back.

My father answers—do I remember him asking if I am sitting down?—and calmly he says, "Dave was in an accident last night." My eyes flick to attention. Dave—about to graduate from Moravian College, twenty-third birthday in a few weeks. Sitting up straighter, I ask if Dave is OK. My dad says, "There was a fatality." A fatality—someone died in the accident. I do not catch on. There is a fraction of empty air, and then my dad speaks one more time, as if apologizing: "Dave was the fatality."

And with that, it's done.

\* \* \*

The moment is inscribed, carved, hacked into the heart, for always. It is a shock so profound that it's almost exalted, a rite, the slaughter of a sacred lamb.

Although we understand the words and we have no reason to think we're being deceived, the news is too sudden, too repulsive. We don't want to hear the sounds, much less understand what they mean. But the sounds, the words, have been spoken or seen. The information is here and we can't unlearn it…but no one can be expected to believe this…it must, *it must*, be a mistake. There is a gasp of thought: *This can't really be.*

The physical reaction is the pulse exploding, the adrenaline flooding, and the breath cut short, but there's no foe to fight and nowhere, no way, to run. Something so drastic and so absolutely unexpected doesn't fit with reality. It isn't anything like coherent knowledge; it's just information that has set off indiscriminate and uncontrollable alarm.

A lamb. Mary had a little lamb. Real baby bundled in blankets fleecy-white as snow. *My bébé*. Little lamb—*Little Shnooks*. This moment is surely not for real?

## CHAPTER 4

# Found and Lost

(Abandonment)

My first coherent sentence in the After-time is this to my father: *Where is he?* As if it mattered. But it does. My dad tells me that Dave is at Doylestown Hospital, and the rest of the family has already gone there, seen him, and returned. They've tried and tried to reach me; they finally had to go without me, and now it's uncertain whether any other visits are even possible. I say that I'll call the hospital; my dad offers to send Tim and Mike to come get me.

Downstairs, the light on the answering machine is blinking. I press the button and hear just one word, in my mother's voice. I never knew my name could be such a dark sound. Her voice is not weak and wavering—this voice is of someone very much aware, oriented with horrible clarity, crying: *"Judy...!"* I can't listen. I press *Stop*. The red light keeps blinking; they've called me over and over. Mindlessly I press *delete-delete-delete*, until all the unlistened-to messages are gone and can't be retrieved.

I lean against the counter and see the strange silent film in my head, see myself falling in slow motion toward the concrete, feel the plunge downward and the shatter of the face, my face. As I stand there, my shoulders hunch up and curl in, like those of a prisoner cringing beneath the blows of a truncheon. I understand that the self I've been, that person in the silent film, will be bludgeoned

repeatedly until it's crushed. But without that self, I don't know
who else to be. There's no choice but to follow a script, play a part,
go through motions. If I want to see my little brother, I have to call
the hospital and get official permission. For the first of countless
times, I prepare to interact with someone who is Not Involved.

Certain allowances will be made for me; it's to be expected
that a victim's sister will be overcome by shock and grief, but even
this latitude is not a free pass. I have to demonstrate that I won't
cause a scene. I have to show that I'm still aware that the universe does not revolve around me. I have to make it clear that
I'm aware people die every day, I'm aware I'm not special, I'm
aware, I'm aware. I do not expect, much less demand, special treat-
ment but am only humbly begging a favor. I must keep control of
myself, because if whoever hears my petition detects a single note
of hysteria, I'll be turned away. Terrified, I dial the number for the
hospital.

An emergency-department nurse speaks to me. She is neither warm nor cold as she explains that they don't usually bring
a deceased person's body back a second time (*Back?* I think. *Back
where?*). It is against standard procedure. I try for calm dignity as
I ask if there is any possible way, it would mean a great deal, is
there any way…it would mean…my voice falters and drops to an
unsteady whisper, but perhaps she hears something within it. Her
own voice softens and she tells me she will bend the rules, since it's
clear that it would be important to me to see him. (*Important* is her
word.) "Yes," I say, agreeing with her, "it is important." I thank her
profusely and hang up. As I shower and dress, I tremble like a sap-
ling, and although I don't know it then, the trembling will go on for
weeks. I take note of myself, as if I were back in medical school jot-
ting down clinical observations of a new patient: *Pronounced whole-
body tremor. Acts with intent, although in significant distress.*

Mike and Tim arrive. I collect my purse and lock the front door, and Mike drives us across town. We pass the metroplex, a sprawl of stores offering home improvement supplies, whole-sale shoes, clothing, groceries, craft supplies, pet supplies, bridal finery, even a guitar store—everything you might need for normal life. Mike quietly remarks that statistics were always against our parents, that with five children, their chances of losing at least one were, it has to be admitted, pretty high. Tim and I murmur consensus; there's no debate, no railing, no protest. Tim is a stat-istician, Mike is a physicist, and my medical degree is four years old. There's plenty of rationality in this preternaturally quiet car. We're all trained to study the natural world, all cognizant that "fair" and "unfair" are human ideas, and that nature is based on matter being neither created nor destroyed but in constant flux.

In flux, like my thoughts, which are random and fatalistic. *The only constant is change*, I intone to myself idiotically. Despite my science-heavy education, my earliest refuge was the non-ra-tional, the borderless right-brain world of books, pictures, ideas, songs, beauty of any kind. A poem by Robert Frost comes into my head, something that has stayed with me from a college literature course and that I think of every spring: *Nature's first green is gold*, the poem says. And I remember nothing more except the last line: *Nothing gold can stay*. Why can I only ever remember the first and last lines? But that's the distillation of it; maybe that's all I need to know. Which then reminds me of Keats's famous Grecian urn from a class in British literature, a poem often quoted with faux sophistication: *"Beauty is truth, and truth, beauty"—that is all ye know on earth, and all ye need to know*. This leads me to think of medical school professors when lecture was ending and they were sharing some last snippets of trivia, raising their voices over the flurry of snapping notebooks and clicking pens: "That's just nice-to-know, people, not need-to-know…exam next Tuesday…"

My mind has clearly gone off a cliff and now it's free-falling down the rock face, and all kinds of bits and pieces are jarring loose on its descent. Needing, knowing, and needing to know, and nothing and no one can stay. There is a brief numbing effect in the incantatory lines, but in a few seconds I remember where I am, where we're going, what the errand is. Our baby brother is dead— for that's how I've begun to think of him again, as our "baby brother," even though it's completely inaccurate and we haven't referred to him or Matt that way since they were toddlers. It's as if to remind the forces of nature that they have unfairly snatched a mere baby, the youngest and most entitled to more time. I stare straight ahead, clutch my tissue, and say nothing. Mike reaches over and pats my hand, for the first, last, and only time ever.

At the hospital, we're met by the same nurse I spoke with earlier. She leads us down to the basement and through hallways, and then to a doorway that opens into a small, nearly empty room. At the far wall is a gurney. On it is our brother, his hair the usual mess of brown curls, his black T-shirt just visible above a blanket. I remember pathology classes in medical school. This thought comes: *Of course they've cleaned him up for the family.* I step into the room and think, *Wait.* There is a small table against the side wall. I move slowly to it and set down my purse, as if this were a preparatory ceremony. I turn and approach the gurney like someone spiritually ready to be executed, carrying nothing.

His face. It's a little swollen, with a scattering of small cuts, a bit of dried blood on each one. He doesn't look injured enough to have been killed. I reach out slowly, as if my hands themselves are dismayed and hesitating of their own accord: *What is this?* I cradle his cheekbones (as if I've damaged something delicate I've been entrusted with, and am now trying to hold the broken pieces together with my hands and pleading, "Wait!") One of his eyes is not quite closed, and a glint of light seems to emanate from it. I want to pretend that he could still be looking out. I take up one of his hands; it's chilled clay. I rest my other hand on his shoulder, wanting to hug him but inexplicably fearful of disrupting him.

Tim, Mike, and I hover there with a sort of stunned gentleness, and we don't speak. Mike uses a small pair of scissors from his pocketknife to take for us a few cuttings of Dave's hair and tiny pieces of the neckline of his T-shirt. Dave's hand, which I'm still holding in mine, has grown warmer—as if it were merely that easy to give back, to revive. (That casual expression has a literal meaning: *death warmed over.*) After a little while, I put down his hand and Tim takes it up. My head drops down against Dave's chest and I look up at his face again, as if sooner or later some faulty mechanism will reengage and he will breathe, move, wake up. But at last my motions stop. My head stays down.

Later, I contemplate the space of time—a few minutes? a half-hour? —that the nurse allowed us. I wonder if she found it strange, a stone-sibling pieta, the three of us dumbly faithful, trying to attend this person we had always attended but knowing he was broken and gone. The first thing we'd done since the day he was born was the last thing, and the only thing, we could do on this day: gather about him and keep him in our midst. It was all we could do so we did it, in a perfect mutual silence that shrieked and tore and bled.

* * *

A human body is heavy and still when its life is untethered, but…the slightly open eye, the warmable fingers, the intactness of a face…all this, and yet the life is gone? We halt in confusion; our hands splay suspended in the air, in an immortal gesture: *What can this be?* Confronting something that defies comprehension, the hands form a shape around the precious lost; they shut out the rest of the world, they frame the thing that can't be believed or grasped, only beheld.

It's counterinstinctive to bow over someone young and dead, especially if we're older than they. Why, of all losses, does the death of a young person incite such primitive objection? This death violates the basic trusts we place in the natural world, in which creatures live out their lives, the older dying before the younger. Instinctively we feel that our life and theirs should overlap, not one contain the whole of the other. Our birth dates and death dates are out of their natural syncopation now. It's not right. We don't just want a younger person to survive; we want to know they'll outlive us.

This is our first glimpse of a transporting loneliness. We may be surrounded by our entire family, twenty friends, a thousand people, and still we're alone. It is the loss of this specific person that no other, however equally beloved, can mitigate. This person's presence is unique, and so is their absence. And this absence—it's not the distance of overseas travel, or the silence of a decades-long feud, or the moonscape of an indefinite coma. It is the only absence that is immutable and total.

Before we bring the dead to their graves or urns or sea or air, we ourselves are abandoned, left in the purest confusion possible. We look, we cling; we try to wake the person up. We become a child again ourselves, a child who hugs and waits in vain to be hugged in return.

In our minds we beg them not to go, as if they are still partly here, as if we are still able to influence what has already happened.

When that doesn't work, we plead for them to return, as if our request might be heard. Our entire being is a simple plea: *Don't leave. Come back. Don't leave us...don't leave me...don't go, don't go... come back...please come back.*

## CHAPTER 5

# First Night

(The Beginning of Chaos)

T im, Mike, and I leave the hospital and go to my parents' house, where Matt meets us on the sidewalk. At age twenty-four he's over six feet tall and solid as a monolith. I reach up to hug him. For a second, he's the only one who can hear me. "Fuck," I say very quietly, an unplanned greeting I've never used before and never will again. I don't worry whether he'll understand it; I know he will.

He says, "Exactly. What the fuck?" This conversation means: *What is going on, and where is he, and who are we, and I can't breathe, and why, but...what the...?What...?*

Indoors, I meet my mother's eyes, which are shot through with scarlet and struggling not to drown. I put my arms around her, noticing that she seems shorter and slighter since I saw her a few weeks ago. I say "Mom" but nothing else, because what else is there? *She is the mother of the fatality*, I think. I'm momentarily afraid this will kill her. I know it won't, but I imagine there will be times when she'll wish it had. Next I hug my father, who carries a towel, holding it to his face instead of tissues. He is ordinarily a very reserved sort of person; the towel and his lack of any attempt to hide it are more eloquent than any speech. In this instant my view of my parents shifts forever. Until now, I've acquired the typical quiet awareness of advancing time, and have

21

practiced the indulgence of quirks and opinions that most adults associate with aging parents. But this is something else again—a sick and terrible pity that ought never to exist. My first sight of them becomes one of the cruelest memories trapped alive in the surreal amber of this day.

It is a day that seems to pitch and roll, drifting away somewhere, nowhere. Relatives and neighbors arrive and withdraw quietly. An aluminum tray of fried chicken that our aunts have brought sits on a counter. There are many friends Matt and Dave had in common; a group of them has assembled in a cloud of cigarette smoke on my parents' back porch. There are whispers as the basic story is repeated like a short news loop: he'd been out at a bar with two girlfriends; on the way home the girls were in the front seat and Dave in the back (was he asleep?); Route 309 southbound. Car somehow out of control; embankment; car somersaulted several times. The two girls survived; Dave was thrown out the back window. Ejected. Police. Crash scene. Investigation.

More details surface later, but for now, there are plenty of unanswered questions and unfinished tasks, all more than sufficient to create the illusion that there are corrective actions available, actions to rectify the situation. The reasoning is simple: a huge mistake, an unintentional Bad Thing, has happened and it needs to unhappen, and if enough of us find the right answer to every question, figure out exactly what transpired, second by second, understand it and reconstruct it, then we ought to be able to reconstruct Dave and fix the whole problem. Every one of us—immediate family, relatives, friends—is in a mental struggle, half aware of the truth, half thinking, *Hold on a minute. Nothing is this bad. We just have to understand what happened and we will clear this up…someone will clear this up. We just have to understand.*

After sunset we end up arrayed on the concrete steps of the front porch, as if we're watching for neighborhood fireworks or the ice cream man. I can't catch my breath and I speak very little. Muteness is a nonviolent protest and also a retreat. To avoid being rude, I make sure to respond gently whenever I'm spoken to, but gradually I also become aware that even if I can't avoid speech, I avoid eye contact as a last resort. I'm trying to draw strength from a makeshift, portable solitude, one created by quietness and averted eyes. My presence means I'm here, but my body language means I'm not here. The profound conflict between these compulsions—the need to be present among others, and the need to be alone—is a high-voltage transformer, processing too much current at one time. Despite my efforts to be warm, perhaps somehow I'm coming across as cold. I'm failing at that most basic of social skills: mutuality. In the currents, a sudden arc: *inadequate*. Then that's gone, too. As the night darkens, my own gaze feels like an empty watchtower, directed to a far distance and seeing nothing. We sit there on the porch steps all night.

Later, I'll be unable to remember how that night finally ended. At first I think this is because my memory simply failed. And then I'll understand that I don't remember because there was nothing to remember. That day and that night didn't have an end.

\* \* \*

We try hard to understand that our loved one is not coming back, but this is still far beyond our comprehension. Instead we stop our own lives, stop everything, and we try to stop time. A poem by Gerard Manley Hopkins says that "each day dies with sleep." By night, a normal day is lost to time, and sleep is trust. To sleep is to put aside our cares, knowing everything will be there to pick up again in the morning. But such a day as this? This day doesn't have the shape, the edges and passageways and limits, of a normal day; it is a fog of time we drift through like wraiths. The thought of sleep does not even occur. By staying awake, we give the day a chance to be wrong...because it still seems possible we're mistaken, or someone is mistaken, and we can't help keeping our eyes open.

And maybe it's not even a mistake but simply a bad dream. As trite as it sounds, we're willing to hope that perhaps our eyes feel open but really they're closed tight, and in the morning we ourselves will safely awaken.

## CHAPTER 6

# Choose

### (Effort and Illusion)

T
he sun has come up, and I get a ride with someone back to my own apartment. I shower, dress, and then drive my own car straight back to my parents' house. It will now be the hub of all activity as the viewing, funeral, and burial planning begin.

We go as a family to the funeral home, which is situated directly across the street from the Catholic church my parents attend. The subdued but reassuringly capable funeral director ushers us gently into the tranquil interior, as if we are overwrought children who need quiet time and maybe a storybook before being tucked in for a nap. We're invited to sit at a long, wide conference table of shining dark wood. The funeral director starts by gathering information for the obituary. My mother is tearful as she answers his questions. The rest of us are quiet, sometimes helping with the answers but mostly just glassy-eyed.

I go to the restroom, which is softly lit, a cocoon within a cocoon; there are flowers and the inevitable box of tissues. I wonder what it's really like, running a funeral home as a career. To be mindful with every decorating detail that "work" means hosting a kind of gruesome party that no one wants to attend, orchestrating gatherings at which all manner of behavior is displayed, heroic or unseemly, vulgar or vulnerable, none of it unique—what inspires someone to such a career? What does it do to a person, over time?

I return to the gracious, gleaming table, where my family's bewilderment, politeness, anguish, and piercing gratitude are entwined and almost visible, like a bizarre centerpiece hallucinated by someone with a high fever. (The gratitude is for the funeral director's strength, which surely means he will help us find our way out of here and back to real life, if we only follow his gentle instructions.) My parents make decisions about the coffin, and the funeral date is set for the upcoming Wednesday. We're encouraged to bring personal items representative of Dave to the viewing. At last the discussion finishes up. Composed and compliant, we file out with our fragile plans, distribute ourselves among the cars, and head back to my parents' house.

Later, I go with my parents to choose a gravesite because I can't endure the idea of them having to do this by themselves, but while they speak with the groundskeepers, I stand back alone under my umbrella. It is raining lightly as the merits of various grave-plots are discussed. We end up at a plot with a small tree next to it. The pathetic appeal in my mom's reasoning—yes, this one is good; "he will have a view of the road"; there is a nice little tree—drags at me like an anchor caught in sunken wreckage. Memories rise up as clouds of disturbed sand, memories of other decisions about what Dave would like, what would be good, what color icing on his birthday cake, would he like a Conehead Sundae at Friendly's, would he like a set of fluorescent-color markers, what would he like to be for Halloween, when shall we have his graduation party?

I'm getting steadily more disoriented. What family are we, what stage are we on, who is watching us say these lines, why are we cast in these roles? And when will we be done with the ill-written charade of "Dave Was Killed"? The activities are beginning to gather a nauseating momentum...*there is a possibility that this is all real*...and it's hard to keep up, being herded and thrust into decisions and at the same time still trying to master the simple reason for it all. But it can't be helped; the groundskeepers are waiting for a final decision. My parents have no choice but to choose.

When Matt was a baby (and often called Maff), Tim studied him for a school science project. The experiment, designed to figure out whether an infant might have favorite colors or patterns, involved a lot of coaxing: "Choose, Maff, choose!" Matt's steel-trap mind took it all in, and thereafter, his baby voice could sometimes be heard issuing a hearty command: "Choose, Tim, choose!" I wish Matt were here, to help choose for Dave. And idly I begin to wonder if Matt can bear the loss of Dave with more strength than Dave would have been able to bear the loss of Matt. Even if it were true, is that something to be grateful for?

And with that, I fall into a livid maelstrom of trumped-up options and what-ifs, the sort of thing I imagine happens to anyone in this situation. What if it had been Matt, or Tim, or Mike—would any of them better withstand the loss of any other? I whirl around in these thoughts for a while, and then abruptly I'm flung out of my own head because I'm being spoken to. Reality is a rainy cemetery. My dad has seen me hanging back and is encouraging me to join them, clearly thinking that I must feel left out, standing there by myself. How would I explain that I want to stand back? I feel like a mauled animal, instinctively withdrawing from touch, but I go along anyway, joining him and my mother at the newly chosen gravesite. I agree with my mother that the little tree is sweet.

I think about my littlest brother. *You were coming back home from college, but you won't go home after all. You'll be here instead. And the thing is, if you heard us saying this spot was nice, you would affirm that the plot we've chosen is yea verily the best one here. You would hasten to validate the specialness of the tree, and immediately it would be unbearable to you to be situated somewhere else, because you wouldn't want to leave the little tree standing all alone in the grass. You'd choose to stay with it, keep it company. Very soon it would acquire a silly name all its own, something endearingly stupid like Leaf-ed Buddy, and there would be general mirth over the hymn-book solemnity of "leaf-ed" and the play on "bud."*

*Where are you?*

The rain continues, and the splotches on the toes of my leather clogs darken as we stand there in the wet, still-anonymous grass.

\* \* \*

The mind is a problem-solver, and when there's something we desperately want that seems out of reach, we don't immediately accept it as a situation beyond our control. We don't see it as a foregone conclusion. No, we immediately see it as a problem, and a problem, we've learned, always has a solution as long as we're willing to work at it. How can we get this thing we want; what can we negotiate?

We can imagine at great length what we would give up from our own life, to have our loved one back. Home, friends, hobbies, dearest possessions, a normal lifespan; those are so obvious they're hardly worth mentioning. We move quickly on to things that might be worse than losing life: we could give up our sight, or all muscle control, or maybe memory. (Could we be given a few minutes to know he or she would be back, before our memory would be erased?) If we gave up all love and happiness forever, would that work? And speaking of penitential sacrifices, if we'd spend our lives in solitary squalor, with no human contact—only rats, roaches, and fetid dripping water—could that earn the return of our lost person? This task is momentarily peaceful, this searching for something more intolerable than the torment we're in now. Our determination to buy back the one we've lost is limitless.

The problem is, sometimes a problem is not a problem at all; it is just the way things are. It's impossible to strike any Faustian bargains now, but that's exactly the one thing we don't want to know. The thing we hate most is seeing that there is no choice. If there is no choice, we'll try to manufacture one. And if the choice is an illusion, we will play along anyway. We'll take what we can get, because we know the saying about beggars—and that's exactly what we are.

## CHAPTER 7

# The Speed of Dark

## (How Quickly Life Is Altered)

S ooner or later we would all end up there, like iron fragments
drawn to a magnet: the place on the highway where the crash
occurred, the place where he breathed last, lived last. It will come
to be known to us simply as the Site.

Relatives and friends crowd into cars with us. Our destination
is a roadside ditch on Route 309, near Telford, Pennsylvania. It's a
random bit of four-lane highway, indistinguishable from millions
of other stretches of pavement and concrete barrier and traffic
going too fast. To get to this place, we have to overshoot on the
northbound side, exit, and get back onto the southbound side. As
we finally come around the crucial bend, there are black marks on
the road—yaw marks, a term I had to look up when the detective
assigned to the case first used it in one of his innumerable conversations with us. It turns out that yaw marks are the visible echoes
of screaming tires, dark swipes burned into the road when tires
roll in one direction and slide in another at the same time. These
smudges on the road help us find the exact spot we're looking for.

We pull over carefully where the grassy shoulder dips and then
rises, and long weeds climb up the steep hillside. There is a scatter
of yellow wildflowers; the trees are green and fresh. The weather is
nondescript, the sky colorless, and the air is mild enough for short
sleeves and jeans. The day is ordinary.

My mother and my aunts are loosely gathered. Tim and one of his friends walk along the edge of the asphalt. We look up and down the roadside, we wonder and consider; we try to calculate and estimate things. Distances, forces, durations. We're deep into figuring-out mode, deep within the desperate fantasy of a different ending. We walk back and forth with slow steps, studying the ground. Strewn in the grass and along the paved shoulder of the road are gum wrappers, cigarette butts, receipts from convenience stores—the detritus of a Friday night out with friends. But there's more. Bits of crushed greenish windshield glass form a glittering tracery half-hidden in the grass, like a swath of uncut gemstones, as if someone had walked by with a hole in his pocket, not realizing all his treasure was pouring out onto the grass. These raw crystals are the sort of thing I would have been entranced by as a child, always on the lookout for sudden sparkles in the dirt, tiny pieces of treasure disguised as trash, overlooked by the inattentive and the careless. And here they are, a trail of glass-crumbs, leading us right to *him*.

We examine the spray-painted markings the police have made on the road, white symbols that are part of the documentation of the crash. A small white *V* has been sprayed at the edge of the pavement here, a symbol, we guess, for "victim." In the grass next to this mark is another white painted symbol, a circle connected to a straight line aimed toward the hillside. It is the most basic possible stick figure, or a quick sketch of a banjo. Dave, the artist of the family, doodled stick figures constantly; Dave played the banjo…but this sketch is only meant to indicate where his body lay when the paramedics found him.

Within the circle representing his head, the grass is darkened with a dull gleam where blood has soaked into the earth in a small unobtrusive patch. My mother stoops down and presses her hand to the grass within the circle. When she stands back up, I crouch down and hesitantly reach out my hand, and rest it softly among the maroon-stained blades.

My hesitation is for what this grass is, because it is the most specific grass in the world. Right here he died, his head bleeding. *The infant's skull is vulnerable; always use care when touching the head.* My eyes squint, and then they close. Deep within my own head, a keening begins. I smooth the grass very lightly and then withdraw my hand, afraid of desecration.

Some sort of time passes, but there's nowhere else to go. The shoulder of the road is just wide enough to park on, but it's not meant for that. By walking back and forth along the roadside, we're creating a distraction for passing motorists and putting ourselves in danger. This fact hangs there like a dimly lit bulb in a noonday sun, pathetically irrelevant. Gusts shove us blindly as cars and trucks hurtle past, but this doesn't remind me of danger so much as it reminds me of speed. How fast everything goes, how fast it all happens. How there must hardly even be time for the breath to be taken, when you feel your life suddenly jerk and slip and then you're taken into upside-down over-and-over-and-over and then dark.

* * *

It happens so fast, the plunge into knowing. And it happens more than once. The death itself has happened only a single time, but for those left behind, the moment of realization occurs again and again.

We learn to take in its meaning, and at the same time we learn to be on guard against it. Each successive thing we grasp for—a last glimpse, an official report, proof he died, proof he lived—becomes in its turn the most important thing, and the frantic search for it will not be denied. Everything must be verified. Knowing it's useless makes no difference; we have to convince ourselves anyway. And when we find the evidence we need, we can't manage it. It's too soon and will always be too soon.

But the gathering of facts, this frenzy of figuring out "how it happened" that seems so pointless, does serve a purpose. Like a patient waking from deep anesthesia who can't believe that ten hours have passed (*didn't I just fall asleep?*), we need to envision what transpired while we were elsewhere. Picturing what happened gives us the reality our minds need in order to make sense of our loved one's sudden disappearance. It's our only way of accounting for a time in which things were happening to *us*, *our* lives—we were losing him; she was going from us—without our knowledge. The sequence of events must be reconstructed with facts, imagined repeatedly in order to be believed, and the outcome has to be re-understood over and over again. And each time, we relive the trauma of finding out.

There is a specific cruelty when it happens like this: By the time you even hear of it, the person is already gone and you can do nothing. There is no warning, no courtesy of fate, to give you a last chance to live *with* that person. There is no final communication—no smiles, no tears, no remembrances, no apologies, no bargains or promises, not even the speechless heartfelt grasp of a hand. You want to save them, or at least say good-bye, but you'll get no opportunity. The person has disappeared before you even know what is happening. The unfairness is stunning but it doesn't matter; there will be no mercy, no exceptions, no appeal. It's too late.

And if ever you think you've mastered it, you'll find your-self still secretly wishing for just one more second with them, just one, it's not much to ask, it's nothing really, what harm could it do, why couldn't you be granted just that one more second? But in every moment of the rest of your life, it will *always* be too late.

In this moment of knowledge, everyone else is still here, nothing else in life has changed, everything is the same except that this one person is simply gone. In a flash we remember their livingness and our own, and in a flash we can perceive the whole of our lifetime, and we know our lost person will not be in it.

In a single moment, we carry the pain of our entire deprived future; we feel the full burden of all of it at once, and we're crushed under its weight. This long-sightedness is too powerful. It's too much clarity, too soon, too fast.

## Chapter 8

# Driven Home

(Self-Care)

O n Sunday night I return alone to my apartment. I sit on my couch, I get up and pace, I sit down, I get up. I'm watching, waiting, counting out the hours since his college art show last Friday morning, wondering how many hours it's been since he last saw our parents that day, hours since he ate his final breakfast, or since he got into his own car, or got into his friend's car, or laughed, or blinked his eyes.

My own eyes are swollen and unwilling to blink. The windows are open and I'm watching the thin dark of nighttime in May. There's no sun marking time in a relentless march overhead; the dark just exists until it's gone. Night is my time to bear everything that happens in the day, time to catch up with the outside world that doesn't distinguish between this Dave and a million other guys named Dave, or other college seniors about to graduate, or other people who got killed early yesterday morning, or other people who have just lost someone. The rest of the world doesn't wait for anyone in particular, which makes my own waiting seem that much more important, as if I'm the only sentry guarding an entire camp.

The early hours come, they go, and then the darkness begins to dissolve. That first hint of pallor in the sky is a signal that I can close my eyes for a little while, as if there is now no danger of an entire night passing without my awareness. I've done everything possible to keep yesterday alive; I've sat at its bedside all night. The night is on its wane now, but the world is still asleep...it's the no-man's-land of time. I'm unaware of where I am, bed or couch or floor. For an hour or two my alertness dims and I don't know where it goes. Sleeping this way is almost like not sleeping at all.

It's morning. In my kitchen. *The Secret History*, the novel I'd been reading, is still turned on its face on the table, untouched since I'd unwittingly lived through the last hours of my brother's life. I ignore the book. I have to keep moving; the viewing starts tomorrow and the funeral is Wednesday. Preparations are in high gear, and kind relatives, friends, and strangers have been shepherding us through hideous pantomimes: arranging a viewing, choosing a coffin, preparing a liturgical service, picking out a gravesite, selecting burial clothes. The bustle of activity, the creative fervor, and the earnest dedication of such intensely sympathetic people—these are comforting, sometimes for entire minutes at a time. Then a jagged fact gouges the thin veil of comfort: we're doing these things for a kid who was about to graduate college. *This is all out of order*, I think. *This is not, according to nature, supposed to happen.*

I've called my friends and told them. My best friend, Cheri, has known me for so long that she is a sister to me, and she knows that all advice is pointless. But others are worried. "You should try to eat," they've said, "to keep up your strength." *Should*, *must*, *ought to*, *have to*. I appreciate the wisdom of this advice, but my appreciation comes from a great distance, as if I'm hearing a siren in a neighboring county—it's an important reminder for other people, but it's really no concern of mine.

The truth, I've discovered, is that I can withstand a good deal of nutritional neglect. I can't eat anyway; I don't feel anything as

vital as hunger. It's as though one of the swings of that truncheon
has crushed my breastbone and buried a shard of it in my throat,
and it's difficult to swallow past it. I have the facts and I have food,
but somehow I can't *metabolize* any of it—there's no way to neu-
tralize the venom of what I know. My mind retches and retches,
trying to reject the lethal dose, to no avail. I'm truthsick.

But I have to subsist. Coffee is OK; that will go down. Other
things I've been able to drink include the following:

1. lemonade
2. Sprite
3. water
4. more coffee

I eat Kraft Easy-Mac macaroni and cheese. Dave liked to eat
that, so—according to the heart's pitiful logic—it's safe and my
own stomach will accept it. The consistency of baby food, it can
be eaten a few spoonfuls at a time, then put back into the fridge.
In addition, Cheri and her parents, known to me for decades
simply as Mr. and Mrs. B, have given me two plastic bags of
cookies called pizzelles. As big around as saucers, thin and delicate, they're made on a kind of waffle iron so that they look like
pastry doilies, or fantasy snowflakes, or cathedral rose-windows
rendered in wafer. They're mildly sweet and dissolve quickly. I'm
comforted by their lack of substance, the way they don't threaten
to nourish me. They're safe too, and I live on them. Eating this
way is almost like not eating at all.

\* \* \*

To grieve is to be ill, and the pain of the mind, like all pain, is felt in the physical body. We never need rest and nourishment more than when we're ill, but it's precisely then that the thought of food can make us sick and the relief of sleep will not come.

When our loved one is gone, deliberately nurturing our own vitality is not only difficult, it's somehow offensive. Somehow it seems to imply consent; it seems to mean that we've agreed to keep living as we always do. How can we? Anything with a sense of "continue" and "normalcy" in it smacks of the onward progress of time, which is one of the simplest, most frightening ideas the bereaved are facing. Even something as natural as day turning to night brings dread. To live through a day without our lost person, and then to live through another day and another, feels like we're leaving him or her further and further behind. So we ignore our nurture-needing self, which is easy to do when our stomach is clenched like a fist anyway. How and why has this death made us so indifferent to our own survival?

Life isn't just about surviving. As adults we know we don't technically need any other person in order to survive physically. We can take care of ourselves; we know what to do—eat, sleep, stay warm, move—to keep ourselves alive. But living is about more than just methods. We need *reasons*. What we have lost is not the means for our own survival but a reason for it. This person was part of what made life good and worth living. Now that they've gone, there is one less reason to engage in our own life, and overnight the prospect of our own death has become less unwelcome.

## CHAPTER 9

# Lullaby

(Escape)

*Down in the valley,*
*Valley so low*
*Hang your head over,*
*Hear the wind blow...*
  —*Anonymous, traditional lullaby*

On Tuesday I go to the dance studio for a previously scheduled lesson. It is my first exposure to people who know me but who never knew my brother. These people belong to my own self's life, although right now I'm stranded in a place where they can't reach me even if they wanted to.

The staff members are kind to me but perhaps they think I'm confused or even delusional for coming here today. They look at me, but I'm indifferent; I don't try to imagine what ghastly thing they must see. I'm not here for comfort. I'm not here to learn or perform, or to be, anything at all. I'm here to disappear. If I can't have *him*, then I don't want *me*.

I ask to practice waltz—a waltz, with head turned firmly away from where the body is going, feet tracing patterns and the whole body gliding through space until I become not a person anymore but simply an object in motion. *A walk is a dance is a lullaby.* With scalded eyes, I allow my mind to blur, to become only rise and fall, sway and swoop and lift, because in this, I'll be carried far away for a long and timeless time, and eventually lulled and finally stupefied into the mercy of oblivion.

\* \* \*

In early grief, slowly and surely we're coming undone. The cry is inside: *I am not in pain; I am made of pain…I don't want to be here; I don't want to be anywhere…I don't want to be.*

Sometimes the best we can do is to defend ourselves against too much knowledge and instead try to forget, for a little while, what's really happening. It's for the same reason people buy cradles and swing sets, rocking chairs and recliners, porch swings and hammocks and gliders, and spend hours pacing the floor of the nursery, the office, the sickroom, the porch: When mere awareness becomes a torment, sometimes only the primitive lullaby of motion will serve. Sometimes only the ancient sensation of back-and-forth can anesthetize an agony as visceral as this.

# Lingering Thoughts
## on Loss

T he first hours are shock and vertigo—everything too much and too fast; too soon and too late.

Shock is a single blow out of nowhere that knocks the unwary straight to the ground. Vertigo is everything spinning and more blows coming, again and again. There is no real day or night.

There is chaos like a predawn fog: we're blinded and defenseless within it, and we can't be sure it's even real. We don't realize that the fog itself is a blessing because for a little while it shields us from what is coming.

But morning won't wait; when the first sunrays of an incomprehensible new day pierce that fog, there is no more hiding anywhere. The ugliest sunrise we will ever see foretells every remaining sunrise in our own lives, mornings that will come bright or soft, grey or gold, but every single one exactly the same: empty of that one single life.

# Salvage

## CHAPTER 10

# Closure

(Social Ritual)

*Parting is all we know of heaven*
*And all we need of hell.*
   —Emily Dickinson, *"My life closed twice before its close"*

The funeral director has warned us discreetly ahead of time that because of Dave's injuries, his embalmed body will not look like him. I wonder: *Who will he look like?* The answer is that he doesn't look like anyone—not himself but not anyone else either. Even his hair has had the curl brushed out of it by a stranger who didn't know what he really looked like, although we've provided a picture. (Later, I more fully appreciate the visit at the hospital. He was already gone then, but he was still real. It was crucial to have been able to see him, hold his real hand, hug him, recognize him one more time before what remained of him was utterly changed.) What rests in the coffin is a doll—half flesh, half wax—and not even a very good likeness. *But still, we don't complain*, I think. *Because soon this will be taken away too.*

At the viewing, a line of people trails out the door and down the sidewalk for many hours. The family talent for hospitality is at its height tonight; we've instinctively spaced ourselves across the entire room to make the greeting process more comfortable for the guests. Tim and Matt are just inside the door, my parents stand at a front corner of the room. I have stationed myself next to the casket, and Mike joins me there. At some moments it feels almost like a peaceful demonstration, or a genteel campaign, or even a benevolent conjuring: *If enough of us assemble, then perhaps...?* But ultimately all that matters is that people are coming.

Some of Dave's friends have difficulty approaching the casket and can hardly speak once they stand before it. A realization is creeping over their faces: death, that theatrical device, has violated their young lives. Mike and I ask each visitor how he or she came to know Dave. The shyest, a young guy who seems overcome with anxiety, at first draws back and declines our invitations to tell us who he is. But we plead gently to know his name; he hesitates, then makes up his mind. Like a wary butterfly in need of momentary repose, he lingers in front of the open casket and he starts to talk about being friends with Dave, and then he gradually edges closer to us, and his face softens and his agitation dissolves, and his words begin to flow. Maybe he's noticed that in fact we're not plying him with social small talk, but instead we're entranced by every word he utters. If he has come expecting to feel only grief and horror, then maybe he'll leave surprised, because he has given us something that we receive as a gift. I remember from attending the funeral of my own friend Kim, years ago—when you know only the deceased, but not their other friends or family, you feel a little bit like a stray cat at the official ceremonies. I imagine Dave would appreciate us seeing to all these stray-cat friends of his, just as I imagine he'd appreciate all of them seeing to us.

We mutely greet our own friends, and Mike observes a peculiar effect: the sight of a personal friend of one's own somehow pierces the armor of playing host. Our own friends' presence is a gesture that says, *You're here because of your little brother, but I'm here for you.* It's the comfort of someone who may not share our specific loss but who cares about us. Just that bit of distance, the slight detachment, makes them figures of strength. They put their arms around us; we can't handle what's happening, but they can.

All through those otherworldly hours in the strange golden hush of the funeral parlor, we smile real smiles. "Thank you for coming, thank you so much for coming," we say over and over, fervently, as if we've thrown a party and are surprised and delighted that so many could attend. A weird party for sure, where people get caught up in talking about him as if he were still around, or laughing at his particular brand of humor, and in the same moment the laughter dissolves—we don't yet have any idea what to do with all these details that belong to this one person we all know as Dave.

After several hours, Mike looks at the long, winding line of people that still stretches out the door and says, "I wish it would never end." But eventually it does, and then the viewing is over for the evening. Because there will be another session tomorrow morning, the coffin lid stays open for the evening. The open lid haunts me, but not because it is open. It haunts me because very soon it will be closed.

To survive the night, I go home and try to write a poem, something to read at the funeral. The effort keeps me occupied all night. I call the poem "Little Bird" and hope I'll be forgiven for all that's maudlin and incoherent about it. It's not finished by next morning so I scribble and revise as I sit in my parked car, and then it's time to go back into the funeral home.

The second viewing session is just like last night; even the lamps are on, although it's morning. Not a single detail has changed, but I'm not fooled. Today I know what's coming.

Soon, the last of the guests are going out across the street and into the church, or perhaps back to their lives, leaving only the relatives still in the funeral home. There is a protocol that guides the ritual of people leaving the room, a protocol evidently based on blood relationship to the dead. When only the six of us are left, something disturbs the trance of all this formal ceremony. It's something like what happens when a very young child, deliberately left behind, perceives that you're not going to return at the sound of its cries. Swiftly the tide rises from surprise to outrage to panic, until finally the child begins to choke on its own desperation. Today, in this certain moment, I've endured everything else, but I can't endure them closing that coffin lid. The idea fills me with a blank white terror. Closure, literal or otherwise, is the one thing above all else that I do not want. As if I were choking, I make no sound, but I fold in half, and Mike keeps me from falling to the floor. When I catch my breath and stand up again, the coffin lid is closed.

It's time to move in procession across the street to the church for the funeral. I have four brothers and I know they're all here, but the image before me doesn't make sense: Tim, Mike, and Matt are escorting Dave's coffin—*coffin? Dave's?*— but there's no time left; they're taking the coffin across the street. My brain is babbling: *Can't they stop taking him away?* My sister-in-law Laura kindly offers to walk with me. In the crosswalk, with cars waiting on either side for our little procession to finish, I swallow back the urge to be sick right on the street, and concentrate on keeping up with the closed box that contains all that's left of my little brother. Another stage of parting is finished and will never come again.

\* \* \*

We rely on the rituals of parting because they happen in stages. Especially if the real parting wasn't gradual, we create a false sort of gradualness by artificially slowing down the departure. With our ceremonies, we parse the going-away into precise steps. Doing this gives us the illusion of having time to make our farewells. Perhaps we shut ourselves down and grit our teeth blindly until it's over...or maybe we cling piteously to any delay.

A transition from the literal to the symbolic starts almost immediately, because it has to. We begin to bypass physical presence and live directly with meaning. Foremost is the viewing of the person's body. Some of us might prefer to remember our last vision of the person in life. Some of us cherish the opportunity to see the lost person once more in any form, no matter how ravaged, to reverence what once housed their life. Some of us get no choice at all. Perhaps all we have is an article of their clothing, or a piece of paper with the official news of their death.

People come to the rituals, either to share their own grief or to offer us support. They might be anxious when attending a memorial service, especially if they don't know the family. There is concern about what to say, because "I'm sorry" seems so trite; they're afraid their words will be inadequate comfort. They don't realize: their presence *is* the comfort. It gives us strength to be with other people who, like us, look straight into the starkness of life without our loved one and acknowledge that this is a bad thing, and adjusting to it is going to be a bad time. Closure marks the end of something that we never wanted to end in the first place.

## CHAPTER 11

# The Significance of Gesture

(Meanings and Risks)

Two things about the funeral stand out to me afterward. One is something we do, and the other is something we don't do.

Before the funeral service begins, the family members assemble in the vestibule of the church, where a folded cloth—the pall—is to be draped over the coffin. The priest and acolytes start to unfold it and encourage us to help them, so we all reach out to smooth it into place. It's very natural, this smoothing motion. You do this with a little kid's hair when they're telling you something that has upset them or thrilled them, or you smooth their forehead when they have a fever, or when they've fallen down and their clothes and hair are disheveled, or when you're simply overcome with how cute they are and you're marveling at the tiny crumb-covered face with its mobile features waiting expectantly for you to supply another bite of birthday cake. The smoothing gesture is versatile and familiar, and to be invited now to help arrange this piece of cloth adds a note of unexpected tenderness to the formal ceremony.

The other thing I remember most clearly isn't familiar at all: unlike any other social occasion any of us has ever attended, we don't even try to put on friendly smiles and hide what's in our minds. We participate in the entire funeral with authentic expressions unmodified by social graces.

Later, we make other unscripted gestures in our attempts to respond to what has happened, gestures just as significant as the ceremonial ones. My parents tell me that on one of their trips to the crash site, they climbed down the side of the embankment along the highway. Neither of them is remotely athletic, and my mother has the proverbial bad knees. I am aghast. "What would you have done," I ask her, "if you'd slipped on that hillside?" "Dad would catch me," she says. I try to envision sixty-year-old Dad "catching" fifty-nine-year-old Mom on a steep hillside beside a highway with no guardrail…my answering laugh is grim with hopeless understanding. I get it, the heedlessness.

Throughout May, I think of this on my evening drives home from the dance studio, several times a week. Part of the drive takes me across an overpass, beneath which is a highway. I've noticed that on the concrete shoulder of this overpass, there is a symbol in white spray paint, probably some sort of indicator for bridge maintenance—it's a small circle and an arrow parallel to the road. Although not exactly the same arrangement, it is made up of the same figures—circle, line, and a *V*—that have been spray painted in white somewhere else. I quickly develop a habit of stopping the car on the shoulder close to this symbol, putting the hazard lights on, and getting out. This is dangerous because it's at the bottom of a hill that has a bend in it, and cars tend to come down at speed. But on these evenings after my dance lessons, I simply stand against the chain-link fence for a few minutes looking down at the highway below.

One particular evening, though, I leave the car further back. I know this spot is meaningless in itself—nothing happened here—but it's above a highway and it's got a white spray-painted circle and line, and these things can't be ignored. Aware that I'm taking a significant risk, I put on the hazard lights and leave the car behind me as I search carefully for the mark on the pavement.

When I find it, I kneel next to it, place my hands down on the pavement, and then I put my face down and kiss the pavement inside the circle, exactly where someone's head would be if they lay there on the road. I know it's ridiculous and undignified, not to mention stupidly dangerous, but this gesture was the right thing to do and the effect is shocking: for a few seconds, everything in me that's ragged and flailing has somehow been gently enfolded and contained. It is the gesture I would have made if only I'd had the chance to say good-bye to my littlest brother, whose infant entirety I had so many times enfolded and contained in my adolescent arms.

We four remaining siblings have already devised plans for the crash site, plans to make a garden up on the hillside, to clear an area and put stones there, and plant special shrubs and a lilac tree and arrange decorations…but these plans, although made earnestly, are half-baked. Some of them happen—a lilac tree is planted, wind chimes are hung on the trees, candles are arranged, and the occasional toy is left at the piece of white fence that happens to be at the top of the hillside—but further developments are not, after all, pursued. The property technically belongs to the Pennsylvania Department of Transportation and is too close to the homes of strangers, one of whom has registered a complaint, saying he does not want to see reminders of death. The highway maintenance staff collects our things, and in a gesture of surprising kindness, they save them for us to retrieve later.

At the cemetery, my parents take meticulous care of the grave, but the crash site itself reverts to a quiet, mostly untended place, with the lilac tree staving off total regrowth, and the wind chimes staving off total silence. Inadvertently the site becomes a memorial to those first few weeks of frantic gestures and half-fulfilled vows, vows whose purpose was to stave off an insanity of pain.

\* \* \*

The gestures we make as part of ceremonies are publicly witnessed and often stylized, things like religious services, driving with headlights on in funeral procession, placing a flower on a coffin, or throwing a handful of ashes into the sea. But there are many other gestures besides the official ones.

We become suddenly indifferent to things that we ordinarily care about, such as how we look to other people. Intense and unremitting pain rearranges our faces—maybe it puts on them the expressions we wore as very young children, when every hurt was intense and we had no skill in hiding anything. In other circumstances, we might cringe to know that others can see us at such a time, but in this instance, it just doesn't matter. The magnitude of our injury plainly overwhelms the usual concerns about social niceties.

If some gestures are in disregard of how we look, other gestures are in disregard of our sense of safety. Although we know the things we're doing might be irrational or downright dangerous, that only makes us perversely more determined to do them. We appear to have lost all common sense. It's as if a grenade has fallen into a construction site, overturning all the proper barriers and demarcations. Warning signs that say HAZARDOUS MATERIALS and DO NOT CROSS and HARD HAT AREA are uprooted and scattered like scrap iron. There are no inspectors; the quality-assurance guards are gone; there's no one overseeing any of it, and we're resolutely salvaging, oblivious to danger.

We might not truly think we'll come to harm, or for the moment we don't care. Maybe we secretly wish we might come to harm. Perhaps it's the devaluation of our own survival again. It's human nature to equate danger with risk, and risk with value.

We know we ought to be careful, but something's been stolen and we'll venture into any territory to steal it back, even if only symbolically. *I wouldn't risk it if it didn't matter. I wouldn't risk so much if I didn't care. I wouldn't have taken such a risk if I didn't think it was worth it.*

The body and mind are connected in a way that disregards linear time. Intellectually we know our lost person is dead and we know our actions can't save him or her, but we go through certain motions anyway—climbing down an embankment, kneeling on a dangerous road, risking harm in order to communicate a message. Even though we know we won't change the outcome, we do the things we would have done if we'd had the chance. When we do this, something strange happens: paradoxically, these "crazy" behaviors seem to have a stabilizing effect. We feel as if we're somehow putting to rights a tiny portion of the unfairness. A foolish gesture becomes something for time and the subatomic particles of the universe to accommodate and record: a formal protest, our defiance of the way things happened.

# CHAPTER 12

# Rescue

(Separation Anxiety)

I've been given one of Dave's wool sweaters, patterned in dark brown, grey, and red, to take home. When I try to go to sleep, I don't clutch the sweater, or hold it like a blanket. Instead, unthinkingly I arrange it above my head, against my hair, as if it were a very floppy sort of hat. I remember something my mother had once told me about myself as an infant, which was that when I was napping, apparently I would scoot around until the top of my head was wedged against the front wall of the bassinette. With the sweater piled against my hair, it's oddly as if I'm back in the world of that infant: the infant who wanted to be aware of something over its head; the one who woke and knew it was alone.

Is this why a residual sadness seems to cling when we wake from a nap? Is it the momentary disorientation, the realization of having been oblivious to the world and a vague feeling that, as you've slept unawares, it's possible you've been forgotten? But the sadness dissipates quickly; another person appears, or you stand up and get a glass of water and hear the TV on downstairs, or see today's mail on the table, and suddenly you're entirely back. Even a baby who wakes up alone in a crib and cries to be brought out is usually consolable, and as a kid I was always eager to liberate Matt or Dave in this way. "He's awake," I'd announce importantly to my mother. "Can I go get him?"

Lifting a baby from a crib is a very simple rescue; I think of how many times I fetched Matt or Dave from their naps, babies fragrant and heavy, with warm, damp hair and flushed cheeks, lolling a little against my shoulder, and often unsmiling. Sometimes, I thought, they looked lost, almost reproachful, as though they'd been betrayed: *You left me all alone up there. You've been having fun down here without me.* Brought down to the kitchen, they'd gaze around fuzzily, reestablishing themselves, not yet ready to talk or play, sometimes not even wanting to be deposited anywhere but instead preferring to be carried around a little while longer. It was a brief, uneasy peace. They'd been rescued; they were not alone; everyone was still there, but the relief always implied a recent anxiety: *Where were you?*

Now, in the aftermath, we try to rescue ourselves by trying to rescue Dave. My parents have requested and received official permission to go to the crash site and dig up the blood-soaked earth from within the white spray-painted circle at the roadside. They bring back plastic bags filled with dirt and bloodstained grass. My dad reassures us that he dug down pretty far in case the recent rain had caused any of the blood to seep further into the ground. This means we can be sure that all remaining traces have been spirited away from there and brought back home.

As I help them set the plastic bags into the soil beneath a dogwood tree in their backyard, my dad describes a lapse in awareness. He says that while he was carrying the shovel to dig up this dirt at the roadside, he caught himself whistling, as if he were engaged in ordinary yard work. His voice has a note of rueful humor; we marvel at the tricks one's mind will play to avoid the truth. We know what it means: the brain tries to ward off terrible things from consciousness, and for an instant, the horror disappears—the fevered mind is spirited away from the ruins of reality, brought back to the sweetness of Before. For a moment I forget the image of my dad on the porch swing on the evening of May 1, in the first hours of his desolation.

* * *

Very early in life, we experience separation anxiety: *If someone I love goes away, they might not come back.* The anxiety is warranted, because an infant without a caretaker will die. But as adults, we function much better if we're not overly preoccupied with worry about whether someone might leave us, or how we'll survive without them, or how they'll survive without us. How do we learn to adjust to separation, then?

As young children, we discover through experience that just because someone is gone doesn't mean they're gone forever. We play peekaboo and hide-and-seek, and the games are fun because we know the other person is only waiting to be discovered. And besides that, the games can end whenever they're not fun any-more. As older children we practice longer separations from our homes: afternoons at another child's house, sleepover parties, a weekend with scouts, or a summer at camp. Over and over again we learn that separations are part of living our own lives, but it's OK because separations are temporary. We learn to "manage" the anxiety because if we think too carefully about all the possible dangers people face in an ordinary day, we'll be eaten alive by that anxiety.

By the time we're adults, we can withstand even a very long absence of someone we're close to, because we assume we'll be reunited even if we have no idea when that might be. What we do, really, is trust that the odds are in our favor. We wave good-bye to a loved person, relying on an eventual reunion. And in the meantime we can reestablish contact with a phone call, an email, or a text message. We've learned to be patient. We understand what separation means: gone for now but not forever. We've learned to trust the odds in order to make the risks of daily life bearable.

But now our trust has been blown to smithereens. We've spent a lifetime suppressing something our infant selves suspected all along: Someone important might go and not return. Eventually, all separations are permanent; we'll abandon or be abandoned, and rescue will not come. As we grew up, we learned to mask that inner knowledge, but now that thing we dreaded as infants has actually happened. Someone dear has gone and will not return. We're alone, out of reach, with no hope of rescue— whatever our age, we're infants again and inconsolable.

## CHAPTER 13

# Pomp and Special Circumstance: Degree Granted Posthumously

(Emotional Confusion)

*I see not his dear little face*
*And hear not his voice in this jubilant place...*
—Eugene Field, "With Trumpet and Drum"

The funeral is over, but the date of Dave's college graduation is two weeks away. Just inside the front door of my parents' house are his computer, art portfolios, and banjo where he'd deposited them earlier last week, and there are many additional bags and crates and books scattered throughout various other rooms. The atmosphere is of arrival, a feeling of transition humming around all the dorm-clutter that has been brought home after four years of transport back and forth. This vivid mess is the essence of college, those flurried years of constant possibility: First semester starts before Labor Day! It's almost winter break! What are you doing for spring break? First year is over, time for a summer job...second year is half over, it's seriously time to choose a major...third year, summer internship, senior year, graduation photo, time to get tickets for commencement...*commencement*, which means "beginning."

The ironies clang like bells falling from their towers and smashing on the ground. My mom has found one of his photo albums in a crate. On its front cover he's written a phrase quoted from ancient Japanese philosophy—*Mono no aware*—with the translation on the back cover: "Beauty of the impermanent." On a closet door hangs the plastic bag containing his graduation regalia, the black academic gown shining in readiness—a perfect funeral bunting.

Because Dave had fulfilled the requirements for his undergraduate degree, we've been invited to attend the Moravian College commencement ceremonies as special guests of a sort. Seats will be reserved for us. Some well-meaning friends have already remarked on how difficult it must be to "deal with" this ceremony after the funeral has already been accomplished. The implication is that I must hate to face such an unfortunate prolongation of pain, how hard it must be, to be reminded.

*Reminded?* The idea is so unintelligible that it might as well be presented to me as a scroll of Sanskrit. This kind of pain can't be prolonged, any more than it can be forgotten. What the ceremonies prolong is his place here among us. I'm *glad* there is yet another ritual that will publicly acknowledge him. It just means the world hasn't quite relegated him to the Past yet. This is the beginning of an eternal confusion: Does his name call up the agony of losing him, or does it call up the comfort of his irrevocable existence? Yes, and yes. We wouldn't miss this graduation ceremony for the world, because although he won't be there, it includes him.

My dad and brothers wear suits, my mother and I wear spring dresses, and we all drive up to Bethlehem, Pennsylvania. The day itself is a glory, sparkling with sunlight and capped with a soaring dome of blue sky. The air is expectant, thrilled, with everyone around us brimmingly happy for themselves and each other. The commencement exercises will be outside—the flowers and greenery are fluttering in the sun, the chairs are lined up facing the stage, the graduates are ceremonially hidden from view, and the guests are settling themselves, clutching their cameras, draping their unnecessary sweaters on the backs of their chairs, eagerly scanning the official program for their graduate's name. Four years' worth of excitement is gathering up for the final triumph. The audience awaits the honored ones.

For the six of us there is just the one detail amiss, and it has turned our day into a glass globe with something stricken and false at its heart. I hold the elegant program as if it were my passport, written proof that I belong here even though I don't belong to any of the graduates. I scan the program and find it: name, asterisk, footnote discreet as a whisper: "Degree granted posthumously." There's probably one in every ten graduating classes, I speculate in my head. There always is. The people around us are strangers, but already they know exactly who we are. It's been two weeks, plenty of time for word of the crash to make its way through the entire graduating class. It's a sick kind of celebrity, as if we are consecrated victims who have inadvertently wandered out of seclusion:

*You know that student who got killed? That's his family . . .*

*Oh yeah, I heard about that—so sad—*

*—our son was friends with him—*

*—our daughter was in his art class—*

*—so tragic . . . how terrible for them . . . can you imagine? Oh, the music's starting, quick, hand me the camera . . .*

First are the introductory speeches and blessings, and then it's time for the formal entrance procession of the graduates. The opening bars of *Pomp and Circumstance* bring the audience to its feet. I'm always choked up at graduations; this one is no exception. But this time, it's not about the impressiveness of achievement. It's about my former self attempting to escape what is happening to it. Each time that self raises its head and claws its way forward, it's grabbed by the throat and flung back. Absurdly trying to rejoice despite all its bloody wounds, the old self finds its voice and fights passionately, truth for truth, with the implacable reality:

*He was just a freshman and now he's finished four years of college; he's earned a Bachelor of Arts!*

He will not receive it.

*But, the cap and gown on the door—*

He'll never wear them.

*I've waited so long to see this, to see him in the procession—*

Why are you waiting? He's not in it.

*Look, they're starting; the first graduates are coming into view. It is so exciting to search out your own graduate in the throng. I'm searching, I'm searching...*

There's no point in searching because you won't find him.

*But...he is graduating—*

No, he's not even here.

*But...his place in line—*

He is not there.

*But where is he, I'm here to see him, we've come all this way; he's come all this way...*

He's gone.

*But everyone is so happy here; this is the day and the place to be happy...*

Not for you.

As the stream of ebony-clad graduates flows out from behind the stage, I remember a letter I wrote to Dave when he was starting college. My mother suggested it and I thought he'd probably think it was hokey, but then I thought, *Who wouldn't like getting an old-fashioned letter?* So I tried to distill for him the most memorable experiences from my own college years and dreamed up which things I'd most wish for him not to miss about his own. Trying not to sound insufferably sage, I told him these four years would career past so quickly that he should savor everything he could. I signed it "Love," which was something we did not typically say to each other. Today, as I recall the things I wrote in that letter, it's as if a hive has been disturbed—each thought flies out fiercely with its own sting:

*Try to know ahead of time how much of yourself you're willing to put on the line for the sake of a new experience...*

*Here is my Be Careful list, which may be old news to you, but here it is anyway...*

*And lo!...try to remember as much of college as you can, because you might give this same kind of letter to someone else some day.*

\* \* \*

No celebration is more effervescent than a graduation. Years of hard work are finished and a long-sought goal is attained at last. People decorate and gussy up, make toasts, give gifts, and take photo after photo of the family's star, the one in the flowing robes, the one wearing the mortarboard that on any other day looks ridiculous but today is a crown of achievement. Everything is black silk and jewel-colored drapery and shiny tassels, with solemnity wafting only half-seriously like a token veil over pure exuberance.

Happy expectations—we must have these to have any ease in regular life. But the more we have, the higher the price we pay when it all goes wrong. When we lose someone, we're enrolled into an education of our own, and we need an Orientation to our disorientation. This is a class no one wants to join, with a curriculum no one wants to learn. Today's lesson: There are mixed feelings that eclipse the mere bittersweet. The accomplishments of a loved one do not disappear when they themselves do. Pride doesn't change, even though the person who earned it is gone.

Imagine, class, that two freight trains are hurtling toward each other, one triumphantly, sparklingly bright, the other so dark that no one sees it coming. The bright one has been gathering momentum for these many years, and it can't be turned aside by any last-minute changes. But the dark one has shown up suddenly, from some unknown direction, and it too is speeding ferociously. There are no brakes and there's no time for any signals. Instead, there is a collision…and what emerges at last is a freakish emotional monstrosity—dark anguish has smashed its way through, but now it's strewn with remnants of demolished joy, fragments of recognizable happiness now in tatters but still brilliant, still billowing, being dragged along wildly, the whole thing screaming along the tracks, sparks flying, all of it unstoppable.

Class, take note, because this is what the entire syllabus is about: This is painpride. Loveloss. Make yourselves some flashcards because there's a lot of material, and it's going to be difficult to get it all into your head, and you'll be tested many times each day for the rest of your life. Sorry, no time left for questions. Study hard.

## Chapter 14

# Sentimental Journey

(The Surviving Younger Sibling)

The graduates are finally seated and more speeches come and go. Then it's time for what everyone's here for: the diplomas.

We've already decided among ourselves that Matt would of course be the one to accept Dave's diploma, so when the roll call gets to the surnames beginning with *E*, Matt slips out of our aisle and waits stageside with the graduates. I watch him standing there in his sport coat among so many black gowns, and I wonder what it feels like.

For each of us, there is the loss-upon-loss, the secondary grief of losing all the others, because their former selves are disappearing too, and can't be saved. A new identity is upon my parents, that of "parents who have lost a child." Tim, Mike, and I are now people who have lost a younger sibling. But although that's also happening to Matt, so is something else, something he must endure entirely by himself. He and Dave literally grew up alongside each other. What must it mean for him now that Dave is gone? Only two years apart, by rights they should have been able to share the rest of life together, just as they shared their youth, and instead—how perfectly unreal must it be?

From the stage, Dave's name is announced, and then the speaker introduces Matt as the person who will accept the diploma. As Matt ascends the steps, all the graduates rise spontaneously from their seats, and in seconds the air is awash with applause. On those waves, my thoughts drift away to twenty-four years ago.

Twenty-four years ago, before Dave, there was Matt: the original bébé whose arrival upended the household and turned it into a circus, and fulfilled my Rosa-inspired wish. He had silky hair like melted dark chocolate and soulful Welsh eyes, and his intelligence was a theme park for the rest of us to revel in. He ingested life in great big gulps, and the single imperative was that his curiosity be constantly fed. His first attempt to say "What's that?" was "Dat-*dat*?"—typically a chirpy question or in some cases a soft query of holy awe, if he were confronted with something particularly amazing. Left unanswered, the query would become an exclamation of increasing urgency, accompanied by hand-flapping and whole-body bouncing: "Dat-*dat*! Dat-*dat*! *Dat-dat!*" he would clamor. This frenzied quest for knowledge would not cease until he received an answer, at which point he would pounce upon the new word and add it like another girder to the fabulous skyscraper of his vocabulary.

It was with Matt that it all began, the whirl of firsts that Tim and Mike and I got to witness, things most people don't see until they become parents themselves: first smile, first teeth, first words, first bobbly little steps, first discovery of electrical outlets, first sight of snow, first attempt to say "lawn mower" and "umbrella,"…first birthday cake, first pair of glasses, first grade. He was the first and last of us who was left-handed. One of my firsts was the discovery that there's no other sound in the world quite like that of a little kid screeching with delight as you spin with him in your arms, around and around and around, fasterfasterfaster—baby Matt even coined his own term, "laugh-scream," to describe the height of hysterical amusement—until a smiling adult reluctantly advises that you slow down. And when Matt heard my dad playing music, I discovered that there's no other sound quite as incongruous as a toddler humming along to "Sentimental Journey," a toddler too young to know the song's lyrics, much less grasp their meaning, but tunefully substituting a nonsense syllable: "Guy ga-guy, ga-guy ga-guy ga-*guy*-guy..." *Gon-na take, a sen-ti-men-tal jour-ney...*

And surely the only thing more entertaining than Matt was Matt upon the arrival of baby Dave. The only family photo I've ever displayed in my own living room is an old one. It's of Matt going on five years old and Dave almost three, a classic snapshot of two little kids in holiday finery. Dressed in matching beige suits with tiny gold buttons, they're standing together against the living room wall. Matt, who's holding a toy car, has his arm slung companionably around Dave's neck, as if the photo were only a minor interruption of a play session. Matt is looking patiently at the camera, but Dave's head of messy curls is turned down because he's busy comparing his own foot to Matt's; you can almost hear him thinking, *Hey, our shoes don't match.* There is an eloquence of baby-loyalty in Matt's casually draped arm and baby-trust in Dave's distraction. It conjures something of the innocent protecting the more innocent, and the indulgence of the young toward the unseen grown-ups, who have been orchestrating such photos since cameras were invented: "Oh, don't you look nice! Go stand over there together so we can take a picture!" Every little kid knows this routine, but they don't know how cute they are—maybe they won't until they're snapping photos of their own little ones. The adults and the little babies play out the imme-morial scenes, with the older siblings as witnesses to it all.

Over the years, we referred to them often as MaffandDave because they were so often inseparable and set apart from the rest of us by nature of their age. They shared and conspired and got into all kinds of trouble together, most of which we'll never know about. But they were separate people, of course…and what can the rest of us possibly understand about the complexities of rivalry and respect, individuation and commiseration, of the particular kind of companionship Matt had with Dave?

I've made this entire sentimental journey in the time it has taken for Matt to cross the stage. But today isn't about saccharine remembrances, putting little halos on kids who were only ever just human beings like everyone else. This moment is another first for me as an older sister: in addition to losing a baby brother, I'm helpless before the loss my other baby brother must now endure in solitary confinement: Matt alone knew Dave so thoroughly; Matt alone lived all but two years of his own life with Dave at his side. As Matt accepts the diploma and shakes the dean's hand, the applause continues, a tribute not just to Dave but also to Matt, for somehow rising to the occasion, for stepping up onto a stage in front of a crowd of strangers, in the midst of a shock and a destruction only two weeks old. He comes down off the stage, passes back into our row, and finally takes his seat. To my amazed eyes, that solitary dignity is the most inspiring accomplishment of the day. How he managed it, the rest of us will never know.

Weeks later, Matt gets a tattoo on his left hand with the dates of Dave's birth and death, and the Latin phrase *Res ipsa loquitur* ("It speaks for itself").

\* \* \*

A brother. A sister. Older. Younger. Much older. Many years younger. A twin; a multiple. A half-sibling, a stepsibling, an estranged one or an only-one. So many kinds of sibling relationships; so little real understanding of any of them. Or so it seems.

The ultimate compliment to a nonrelative is to say he or she is "like family." Close friends may earn this ultimate compliment: we might say they're the sister or the brother we never had. Fraternities and sororities by their very names try to represent this kind of bond. Aspiring members willingly undergo hazing—an entirely manufactured stress—in order to cultivate intense loyalty among each other. Similar bonding occurs in many other initiation phases, from academic programs to religious groups. And the experience of combat, generally acknowledged to be a trauma so extreme that noncombatants can never fathom it, is translated to us with a very specific analogy: soldiers are called brothers-in-arms. What gives the sibling bond its reputation for the fiercest mutual loyalty? Or, for that matter, the most shocking Cain-and-Abel betrayal if the bond goes wrong?

It might be easier to define what a sibling bond *isn't*. It isn't the biological bond of parenthood. Siblings aren't typically responsible for each other's survival, and don't typically suffer the anxieties or the self-sacrifices that go along with that responsibility. And there's no evolutionary compulsion about having a brother or sister: from a strictly biological standpoint, parents need children in order to perpetuate the gene pool, and a child needs parents for physical survival, but siblings don't need each other. In fact, they might even be a threat to each other's survival if resources are scarce. Competition (for parental attention, for supremacy when dessert portions are being doled out, for achievement in sports or academics or arts, or for enough soup when there's not enough money to feed the whole family) is common between siblings, and somehow has to be negotiated if the sibling relationship is to survive.

A sibling bond is a loyalty without authority and without biological imperative, which may be why it doesn't always gel. When it does, the sense of mutual guardianship is voluntary, like a platoon of infantry that chooses to stick together even if given the chance to be relieved of front-line duty. Bonds form among soldiers who live in peril together and protect each other with their lives, in situations of disorder, violence, isolation, suffering, confusion, and an overwhelming need to survive. Their bonds are forged in a foundry whose intensity is likened to another battlefield: the crucible of childhood. It's a revealing perspective on being young—not the watercolor image of graham-crackers-and-milk that we're conditioned to apply to childhood once we've escaped it, but the reality: negotiating a world in which we have very little control (over ourselves or others), no experience, and an all-consuming need to survive.

As adults we may forget how much of our youth is pervaded by fear and frustration. When we're little, we're at our most vulnerable to harm, whether intentional or accidental, yet we have no power and can't protect ourselves. Childhood is a life of extremes: the good is wondrous, the bad is catastrophic, and underneath it all is a terrifying uncertainty—*Today is endless, will there be a tomorrow, and what will be in it? Will I ever grow up?* Through all this, our siblings are right there alongside us.

If childhood is acknowledged as a trial by fire, then maybe that's why surviving even part of it together is the image soldiers use to explain their bond. Adults can recall many years and many memories before a child was born, but siblings inhabit *each other's* earliest memories. Although our parents live with us from the time we're born, a sibling's formative years—their confusion and struggle and all their unrepeatable and starkly emblazoned "firsts"—unfold much more closely in parallel with our own.

It's true that we can share youth and growth with our friends, and sometimes the closeness between friends supersedes that between siblings, but still, our friends come from different families. Why would it matter? Maybe the significance lies only in a certain primitive recognition: something genetic like the same face shape, or learned behaviors like how we move our eyebrows, or the common store of memories involving the same cast of characters and places—same parents, same neighbors, same pets, same kitchen, same family history—that we amass over the years. Ultimately the sibling bond grows from the mutuality of origin *and* experience. Our friends share experiences of growing up with us, but friends don't live with us every single day or go home to the same place at night. Our parents live with us day and night, but they're already grown up. The only person who can truly share all those things with us? A sibling.

For many siblings, there's literally no such thing as life without each other. Unless our sibling was many years younger, we may have only a few memories that don't have our brother or sister woven into them. If our sibling is close to our age, then we two go way back, all the way back. When we lose a sibling, we undergo an often silent devastation, something that takes us apart so completely that we don't even know who we are without them.

As a bereaved sibling, you may be a helpless witness to your other siblings in breathless pain. You may be a helpless witness to your own parents—parents whom you see now almost as if they have become children before your very eyes, children in a dark torment they cannot bear and you cannot soothe. You may feel profoundly lost, and shocked, and alone, like you're not yourself anymore but instead some stranger in a life you don't recognize.

Your relationship with your own brother or sister may be mysterious to other people, and sometimes even a mystery to you. You knew things about each other that no one else knows. Or maybe you always wished for a better relationship but never had it. When you lose a sibling, other people may not understand the vastness of your pain, and maybe you don't even understand it yourself. Your sibling relationship reaches so far back into you that the loss breaks the tender young heart of your deepest childhood self. Without words, that childhood self calls to the lost sibling: *There is no me without you.*

This grief is shattering, unique, and brings intense loneliness. But it also means something else: you have the honor of being the sole guardian of that mysterious bond. It is like a one-of-a-kind lamp you and your sibling carried together. It's heavy to carry it alone now, but you're the only one who can do it.

Two siblings—the same dice, thrown twice.

# CHAPTER 15

# White Rabbit

(Coincidence and Symbol)

May seems designed this year. There is Mother's Day, of course, and later in the month is Dave's birthday. No one has any specific idea of what to do, but we have to do something. Tim, Mike, Matt, and I buy a locket for our mother, and we put a tiny photo of Dave in one side and a strand of his hair in the other. We present it to her on my parents' back porch, which has become the unofficial gathering spot during this bizarre season.

The back porch has thousands of random memories attached to it; the very worst in my own memory is the day of the baby rabbits. The first time we discovered a wild rabbit's nest in the backyard, I was about eight years old and driven nearly to distraction by the temptation to pick the newborn bunnies up, despite the knowledge that the nest must not be touched. Instead, we studied it, the bits of grey fluff mixed with dried grass that formed a little cap on the hole in the ground, like a warm comforter on top of the babies. One day, when one of the rabbits climbed out from under the comforter and escaped, we delightedly assumed the responsibility of retrieving it and putting it back in the nest where we thought it belonged. Another popped out; we fetched that one back too, not realizing that it was simply time for them to venture out on their own. The retrieval process allowed the unheard-of privilege of holding the truant rabbits—was there ever anything so tremblingly tiny and warm, so long-eared and silken and downy, with surprisingly strong little hind legs, eyes the color of midnight, with an ever-sniffing pink nose and an unspeakably frantic heart?

Eventually all but two left the nest, so we brought the orphans into the house, put them in a box, and tried to raise them. We failed. Despite everything we did, they fell slowly onto their sides, and never got up. Our passionate wish to save them and our absolute inability to do so made me sick and silent. After the torturous hours finally gave way, we carried them in a box out to the back porch, dug a grave in the grass, and buried them.

A few years later, the front porch was the stage for another baby-rabbit drama. One of that year's litter had run into a hole in the side of the concrete steps. All afternoon we tried in vain to coax it out. Gradually everyone gave up, but the idea of the rabbit dying alone haunted me so deeply that I wandered back to the front yard by myself, unable to join the backyard picnic, and I kept watch on the little hole at the base of the concrete steps. We'd strategically positioned a piece of carrot as a lure, but that rabbit would not take the bait and thus free itself. At some point I went inside for a bathroom break, and when I came back, Dad and Mike confirmed that, guess what, the carrot was gone! Which proved that the rabbit had come out and run off safely!

More than twenty years passed before it occurred to me that this was probably not true. I never asked, because the lie had been a mercy. But rabbits and porches and anguish were to return once more, along with the knowledge that even twenty-five years is no preparation for the strangeness of some things.

Matt has explained to the rest of us that the white rabbit from *Alice in Wonderland* amused Dave, who every now and then would spout "White Rabbit!" apropos of nothing in particular. And so it was fitting that it happened to be Matt and his friends who were on the back porch together, one day after the crash, when the peculiar event occurred. As they sat quietly smoking in the early morning hours in this nondescript suburb, they looked up and saw, meandering implausibly along the side of the street, a white domestic rabbit.

The stunned group decided the owner was probably a guy who lived several houses down the street. They fetched the rabbit and brought it to this man, who said, yes, it belonged to his daughter, but since no one in their household had any real interest in the rabbit, would Matt like to keep it? Thus there came to my parents' house the only four-legged creature ever to be kept as a pet there, allergies and constant chaos having always made furry pets impractical. But this was, of course, different altogether. *This* was acknowledged immediately and incontrovertibly as White Rabbit, amidst a fascination that bordered on alarm over the undeniably staggering coincidence.

A hut was duly constructed and decorated, and over time, my parents learned its favorite foods, how to interact with it, when to bring it indoors, and how to entertain it by taking it out of the hut for a walkabout in the grass. A visit to their house always entailed a trip out to the backyard to pet White Rabbit, offer it a bit of carrot, and always to gape anew at the fact of its existence. Here was something warm, living, and all unlooked-for, something that needed nurturing, something on which affection could be lavished; here was a creature that had appeared just when another—the very one who made the rabbit significant—had been lost. Here was something that could speak no explanation but whose appearance that morning seemed as eloquent as a mother returning to a child who weeps alone, thinking himself abandoned: *Did you think I was gone? But look: I'm right here...*

My parents tended it to the end of its natural life, which came about two years later. With poignant regret we buried it in the backyard, and maybe it was absurd, walking across the lawn in a kind of procession, but who cared? It had been impossible not to cherish this little white fluffylove of a rabbit. And it was also impossible to think of it in terms of its dying. It hadn't been here long, but how astounding that it had come to us. How uncanny that it had come just then...a *white rabbit, walking down the street?*... how desperately lovely that it had come at all.

\* \* \*

For a certain person to have lived exactly when he or she did...with us instead of anyone else...and the idea that this person lived at all...how desperately lovely.

## CHAPTER 16

# Not-To-Do List

(Attention and Distraction)

After the graduation, my two weeks of bereavement leave from the office are over. I return to work, but telling myself "Concentrate!" is somewhat like telling a chef he must continue to cook after he's been shot in the chest. He can still hold his head up, right? And there's nothing wrong with his hands, as far as anyone can tell. It's the dinner hour and the customers are hungry, and if he doesn't feed them, they'll find someone else who will. He can be easily replaced, so the important thing is to wrap up the wound, let the healing process begin, and keep working, ideally without bleeding all over his work.

After a month and a half of this, I realize I can't continue, but it's unorthodox and risky to declare a need for more time alone. A leave of absence is a privilege, something I wouldn't even be able to consider if I had a family of my own or a less steady income. I contemplate the sheer outrageous luxury of it: to mourn undistracted. As I fill out the paperwork explaining that my grief has outlasted its allotted two weeks, I'm conscious of my great good fortune.

Phone calls come from all levels at the office. The concern is genuine: Am I depressed? Am I very sure that spending time alone is the best thing? Am I sure that dwelling on this is healthy? Have I thought about...well...medication?

Maybe I'm considered too responsible a person not to have discreetly tidied up the spills of my private grief and gotten myself under control by now. I wonder if I've crossed some unseen line between decorous sadness and worrisome fixation, and have now become someone who needs to be talked down from a brink. If I'm away for a few weeks, trying to adjust to this—indeed, dwelling on it is precisely the point—does that mean I'm too fragile and must be rescued before I go sliding off the bell curve of normality?

I answer politely, trying to focus on the genuineness of the concern and nothing else. I readily concede that I am most decidedly officially clinically depressed. I haven't yet learned to stop letting it bother me so much. I think: *What is "letting"? What is "it"? What are we talking about here, a pesky swarm of mosquitoes? Perhaps someone can suggest a good grief-repellent?* This all stirs a primitive urge to lash out, to make an example. In my thoughts, I'm cruel: I want to ask people to imagine that tomorrow there is a phone call saying someone young and precious to them has been killed...I'd make the scene as real as I could, paint the picture with horrible colors so they'd feel it for just an instant: *Just try to imagine it happening to you...you can't do it; you'll shy away from the images, you won't be able to follow the story through, because even when it's real, it's impossible.*

I don't say these things, though, because I don't really want to hurt anyone. Swiftly my cruelty gives way to envy—*You still have your loved ones*—and remorse—*I'm glad you don't have to comprehend this*—and back to weariness. All I really want is for others to respect my own condition, my certainty of what I have to do to endure it. I haven't "moved on"; I'm not moving anywhere. My entire life is paralyzed. I wonder: is it really so difficult for people to believe that my little brother was *that* important?

* * *

When someone is in mourning, the natural inclination for concerned friends and colleagues is to want to hasten the recovery, to promote healing, to foster a return to "wellness" and peace. For many of these well-meaning others, it doesn't happen nearly fast enough. They may even think we're resisting the recovery process, because they can't see any signs of improvement. The pain of loss isn't like a broken leg in a cast or a heart attack that leaves the patient on a respirator; the injury can't be measured with an instrument. To others it may seem entirely mental, or even somehow voluntary. It's tempting to wonder why the grieving person doesn't become more Proactive About Healing: *Isn't it best to get back into the routine of your job? Isn't that the best escape, to distract yourself so you'll start to forget the pain? Isn't it the best thing, to force yourself to accept that death is part of life and just "let him go"?*

But here is the thing: most well-meaning others in our lives are not in mourning themselves. This particular death is not cutting them personally into pieces; it's not shearing their days into bloody little slivers. They don't close each day with the knowledge that (1) everything's not getting better, and (2) the loss is not diminishing. Their regular lives have resumed, and their pain, which is vicarious, is getting better. Our regular life is gone, and our pain, which is relentlessly personal, is getting worse.

It's like trying to ignore a screaming baby after it has been injured. It knows nothing of manipulation or tantrums; it's screaming simply because it's in pain. That screaming can indeed be "ignored," and you can give an excellent impression of resisting the noise. Perhaps you're the parent, perhaps just the babysitter; you can try doing your homework or your online banking…but the likelihood of making mistakes is higher. You can try to watch

TV or go to sleep, but the likelihood of getting any relaxation is
low. You already know the only real way through the night is to
tend to the creature, go to it, pick it up, be there with it, hold it
in your arms while it screams, and eventually, much later, it will
wear itself out. *Then* you can get back to what you were doing
with true attention. *Then* you can "get on with your life," although
you'll be a bit worn out yourself. And don't forget: A traumatized
infant doesn't heal overnight. There will be many more nights like
this one before you can hope to get back to that so-called normal
life. For the near future, this *is* your life, even though you didn't
ask to be given charge of an injured baby. No one ever does.

And none of us knows, until we face the situation ourselves,
how much time it will take us to make the thousand adjustments
we need to make. Facing a death means encountering all the
aspects of life that must be shifted around and changed, or protected from change, if we're to go on. That means we have to
consider everything, from how we set the table to how we plan
our holiday shopping to how we can no longer text that person
when we hear their favorite song on the loudspeaker when we're
at the supermarket. We do our best to face each detail one by one,
completely against our will. Every adjustment we try to make
is an outrage to the inner self. The task is as un-doable as people
imagine it to be, when they allow themselves to think about it at
all. And we can't do it all at once, efficiently. There will be plenty
more pain in the weeks and months and years to come. We can't
put this task down or let it go, any more than we can set down
our stomach for a while when it hurts at an inconvenient time, or
leave our head at home because we don't have time for a migraine,
or put our lungs into perspective and move past them when our
bronchitis is getting on people's nerves.

It's no wonder no one wants to think about it. This new life
is sickening. And learning to live it is a process that follows an

inscrutable timeline. It can't be rushed to suit anyone's wishes, not even our own. The adjustment process can be dulled or drawn out, sugar-coated or stifled, it can be suppressed-facilitated-complicated-avoided-supported-shared-medicated...but it can't be denied.

## CHAPTER 17

# Unspoken

### (Vigil)

My mother is the only one of my family of origin who has already lost her own mother. She can't share this thing with her mom, can't call her with the primitive need to speak a child's words: *Mom, something bad happened...* Her mother isn't there to listen, can't give her a long understanding hug or even a stilted self-conscious one, can't come and help her, can't make her some tea or simply sit in the terrible dark with her. As far as female support goes, there is only one other woman who is floundering in a nearby darkness—not the same darkness but something within speaking distance. Since that first day of May, my mother calls me every night for six months. After that, she calls every Friday night for six more months.

We develop a tacit agreement that the phone conversations on Friday nights will extend past 1:45 a.m., the official time of his death. We ponder the crash—we're not afraid to ponder the crash, and in fact we would ignore any attempts to divert our attention from it. We clutch at the vague comfort of knowing that although we hadn't known what was happening, we'd both been awake that night—she'd stayed up unusually late to watch a movie and I'd been up reading long after I could have gone to bed. (As if that made any difference.) In one of our conversations, she tells me she has gone to Wawa and seen pumpkin seeds with the brand name "David"—we discuss the significance of this. We visit other topics too, such as what the police will say and what the investigation might reveal. (As if that makes any difference.) I mostly listen during these conversations, for she has a need to speak, and I'm nearly unable to. But each time the phone rings at midnight and I pick it up, I've already said the most important thing: *I'm here too*. The sharing has already been done; it was lived.

Our lives have always been extremely different except for one thing, although that one thing isn't motherhood. She is a mother and I am not, but I'm the only other female family member who lived in the same house with Matt and Dave. For her, the sympathy of other female relatives and friends, mothers all, seems to reside at a certain distance because, infinitely lucky, they still have all their own kids. And among the many bereaved mothers who empathize with my mother perfectly, that empathy is somehow a fortune in the wrong currency. These women understand exactly how she feels in an abstract way, but they have no idea how she feels having lost this particular person. The only other woman with a clue about what this particular Dave's mother has lost, is this particular Dave's sister.

My mother is the one who gave me the clue in the first place, by encouraging my role as a mother's-little-helper. Possibly the only significance of that is bound up in the countless hours of routine caretaking tasks, the unremarkable stepping-stones more so than the big moments, for which I was simply there as a girl, alongside her. She let me tend and fawn over her own children, and the years have now come full circle—by sharing that with me, she has enabled me to share this now, with her. With the ritual phone conversations, she and I wander through desolate places, each holding up a lantern in search of someone who has gotten lost. We're not in the same place, but we can hear each other, and we're holding these lanterns up not just in search of him but also for each other. It is an unanticipated reprise to the role of mother's-little-helper, a reprise no daughter ever expects to make.

And yet somehow it has never been entirely unanticipated. On one of the days just after his death, as I'm getting into my car, she comes out to the street to say good-bye. I say, "I was always afraid something like this would happen." The words are very quiet, but she's heard me, and she says, "Me too." And that in itself may have been the single most significant, if unspoken, understanding we've ever shared in the past twenty-five years.

* * *

We're not going to get our lost person back. But it will be a long forever before we stop trying. We're like starvelings who scrabble in the dirt, sifting frantically so as not to miss any stray morsels. If we gather up enough crumbs, perhaps we can assemble something whole.

Sometimes, not having to explain ourselves, not having to give the background, not having to furnish the innumerable and very precise details of the person we're trying to find, is a relief like no other. We needn't say a single word about the one we're looking for now, or about all the prosaic days we spent looking after them in the past. The person scrabbling and sifting alongside us already *knows*.

## CHAPTER 18

# The Work of Breathing

(So-Called "Griefwork")

The leave of absence from work has been arranged, and summer begins. I spend hours alone on my front porch, struggling with my self-help books like a dutiful pupil who can barely read.

The books say, "When we are grieving, we wonder if it will ever stop hurting. We ask, will it ever get easier?" I find that I'm not wondering this at all. Pain is irrelevant because it's not the real problem. The real problem as I see it, the *only* problem, is his absence. I'd endure the pain gladly for the rest of my life, if he would just come back.

Of course this is nonsensical. But the books seem equally nonsensical, reassuring me that I will "feel better" even though he'll never return. If I never get him back, then feeling better is an illusion. (Later I turn out to be partly wrong; I'll eventually feel better in a general, overall way. But I predict I'll never feel better *about this*, and I'm right—I never do.) I don't want to get through the pain; I want to outlast it until he comes back. But panic follows me like a bloodhound, rounding on me without warning, over and over: I can wait, try to outlast anything, but my little brother will never come back.

To defuse anxiety, many books advise, it is useful to begin with the practice of simple breathing. This technique has a primitive appeal to it. Breathing is our first instinctive action as newborns and it grounds us in our very life. In medical school, there were lessons about the physics of how humans breathe. The diaphragm and other muscles, like the tiny ones between the ribs, work ceaselessly, contracting and expanding in order to keep the lungs filling and emptying. The amount of energy the muscles need to use, whether it's a little or a lot, is called the "work of breathing." Right now, there's absolutely nothing wrong with my muscles or my lungs, but breathing is surprisingly difficult and as it turns out, there's only a dubious comfort in paying attention to it. True, it's sort of hypnotic to remember that breathing is our very first instinctive action as newborns, blah blah blah…but on the heels of that thought comes another: Slow, calm breathing is a reminder that *he* is no longer breathing at all. My own breathing calls my attention to the fact that I'm alive and he's not. And I myself am not wholly breathing either; it's painful to take a full breath. What my lungs are doing is better described as making a shallow exchange of air, with many moments of suspended time, as if undecided about fully living.

When I'm tired of being aware of my own breathing and I can't read any more books, I look at photos of my brother. One day I'm looking at a picture of him holding up his paintbrushes, when a slight breeze whisks the photo from my hands. Falling in a perfectly vertical position (what are the chances?), it slips right between the porch floorboards and disappears.

I fetch a flashlight. If I crouch down with my face to the boards I can see the photo down in the dirt four or five feet below. Unperturbed, I go in to the kitchen to find my all-purpose twine-ball, snip a long piece of string from it, grab the duct tape, and get some tweezers. Back out on the porch, I wrap a loop of duct tape inside-out around the end of the string and slowly lower it between the porch boards. But it won't attach strongly enough; the picture keeps dropping back to the dirt. Next I chew a piece of gum and then stick that on the end of the string; still no luck...not with peanut butter either. I fetch a marshmallow and, as I used to do when I was a kid, twist it around in my fingers until it's semi-melted and stretches like taffy. I apply it to the speck of gum that's still attached to the string. Once again I kneel on the porch, my face against the floorboards, and ease the string down. Suddenly I'm in a fragile bubble of merriment, wondering just how peculiar my behavior must look to people driving by, as if I'm ice-fishing on my front porch. I guide the string all the way down and nudge the wayward photo with the glob of taffified marshmallow. The marshmallow lure, which has been given heft and power by its core of chewed gum, touches the photo gently, sticks fast, and a test-pull on the string shows that it will hold.

I reel the laden string back up, tweeze the photo up through the floorboards, and study it exultantly, aware how easy it is to trump up meaning here. I'd once had a white stuffed cat named Marshmallow Kitty, which Dave had eventually appropriated for himself. The toy is now so grey and threadbare it's barely more than a net-covered, stitch-marred wad of stuffing, as befits a twice-beloved toy cat. And now with marshmallow I've managed to retrieve my little brother holding his paintbrushes—Dave would have appreciated this. Would appreciate. Would have appreciated.

The fragile bubble bursts. The truth is here again; the Davelessness is real. I'm still kneeling on the floorboards, chasing the image of comfort through the mirror-halls of memory, but it gets away from me. *Why can't it just be true for part of the time, and not true for the other part, to give us a chance to get used to it?* I'm still breathing, my survival instincts are fighting, but the work of breathing is painful enough to take my breath entirely away. The need to live, and the need to escape what this life has become, are fighting for possession of me.

\*  \*  \*

We hear a lot about "griefwork." It is, apparently, the task we have to do in order to integrate the loss, whatever that means. Griefwork sounds like homework, like lifework, something lengthy and stepwise and big. It is another kind of mastery, and it takes time—and many mistakes and confusions—to process our grief. But what does that mean, to "process" it?

We read pamphlets or get counseling to understand what grief typically entails, so we can understand how it will affect us and be prepared for the extreme ways we will feel. We review the list of the classic five stages, general types of feelings we're likely (although not guaranteed) to encounter. We know denial and disbelief—sometimes we wish we could take refuge in these more often. Anger—we learn that it fends off pain about as well as a clothesline fends off the wind. Bargaining...depression...acceptance—does it count as acceptance if our intellect alone will bear the facts? The world of grief is everything the books say it will be. But these things don't tell us how to navigate the moment-by-moment process of remaining alive when our loved one is dead.

The deeper allure of books is that they can inadvertently foster illusions about the point of doing the so-called griefwork. There's nothing more captivating than the idea that This Won't Last Forever, and books encourage that we can "get through it." There is a cruel hope in that word "through," because it must mean there's some sort of other side, an end, if we can just hang in there. The books are talking about pain, and they are trying to reassure us that the *pain* of loss won't always be so intense, whereas we are concerned with recovering not from pain, but from *the state of loss itself*—and the only one way to do that is to regain what we've lost. We turn the pages of our books intently, looking for symptoms that match our own, because that means someone has researched and understood our suffering, and can tell us how to cure it. We need all the support and advice we can find on how to endure this period of mourning, so that we can eventually emerge on the other side, where life rights itself and our loved one returns.

Ah, no…no. Our loved one will not return. In relearning it, we have to stop what we're doing and catch our breath again. And for this we need an extremely simple guide. Don't resist the feelings, we're advised; let them occur and "move through" us. Or was it that we ourselves should move through the feelings? Move through the feelings, sit with the feelings, contain the feelings, don't try to contain the feelings—what is all this supposed to mean, anyway? What exactly is it that we're trying to do? Eventually it becomes clear: In the simplest of terms, we are learning to succumb to overpowering pain without completely stopping our own breath. Griefwork is the act of dying alive.

How does anyone do that? Maybe the first thing is not weeping or remembering or talking or thinking, but *this*: to accept the body's unwillingness to breathe, despite its need to keep breathing. To allow for the pain, and the exhaustion, of merely breathing. The body in grief is in conflict with itself. Breathing means life and awareness. Not breathing means death. The survival instinct says: *I must not die*. The staggering pain of loss insists: *I can't live*.

As this conflict rages, we might be unable to master something as basic as drawing a full breath. We may have done a better job as newborns. But our lives are at a low point now, so we can do only the minimum: we breathe, however poorly, in whatever way we can, trusting that something will change. Either our loved one will return, or our body will take over when our inner heart fails.

## Chapter 19

# The Butterfly Is Catching Me

(The Mystery of Older Siblinghood)

*It is such a secret place, the land of tears.*
*—Antoine de St. Exupéry, The Little Prince*

July dissipates in volumes of heat. Nothing happens most of the time, although things carry on around me. One evening, I sit so still for such a long time, folded up into a ball on a lawn chair in the driveway, that a skunk walks right underneath me. Maybe I don't register on its senses as a fellow living creature. (It certainly registers on mine.) I'm motionless, amazed.

On a different afternoon, I'm standing on the front walkway in sunlight when a butterfly settles on the brick path at my feet. It opens its wings and begins to sun itself. Slowly I kneel to watch, carefully collapsing all the way down with my arms folded upon my knees. I expect that my movements, however slow and careful, will scare the butterfly away, but I'm wrong. I lean down so close to it, less than two feet away, that I begin to memorize the pattern of its colors: dark grey, red-orange, beige. As it gently exercises its wings in the warmth, some minutes pass, and a few more (again, amazed), and then I lose track of time…and still neither of us shows any signs of leaving.

I'm watchful but calm. Typically I'm repulsed by creatures with six legs, but butterflies are the natural exception, enchanting as oriental fans fluttered by tiny geishas. Of course they're overused as symbols of optimism, happiness, excitement, and transformation, but who cares? They're little flights of delight... which is why it was a source of amusement in the family long ago when baby Matt panicked one day after a moth flew into the car. Strapped in his car seat and unable to escape, he cried out in genuine alarm with what became one of the family's most legendary quotes: "The butterfly is catching me!" We laughed many times over it—after all, what could possibly be more benign or more welcome than a butterfly? What is there to fear from something so beautiful, ephemeral, and so anxious itself to remain uncaught? And how cute of little Matt, naively unaware that of course butterflies don't catch us; we catch them.

Here on the brick path, the butterfly eventually gets its fill of sunlight and flits upward, and as it goes, I stay very still, anticipating something that's never happened before: this butterfly is going to land on me. And it does, alighting on my right shoulder so gently that for a moment I'm unsure. But it's there, and it's walking—I can feel the tiny, otherworldly patting of those miniscule feet. I'm flattered and unaccountably afraid, as if it were too astounding to be borne, because of course I've immediately attached all kinds of significance to this butterfly. *Otherworldly*. In a fear-shot awe I turn my head toward it—and there it is, for all the world as if it were looking at me. The glimpse is a long one, enough for me to acknowledge its presence, to verify its innocent trespass on my shoulder. Just for this instant, the butterfly is standing on me. Natural restlessness lifts it up then, and it zigzags unhurriedly away.

I remember: I'd been a young girl with a young girl's fervent dreams of loving a "real" baby. And one day, instead of playing with my dolls, I held out my arms to receive baby Matt and then baby Dave, and it wasn't a little girl's game anymore, not ever again. For a girl to carry a baby around every day, to cradle its warm head and guard its miniature ribs, to feel its unsteady chin and the innocent trespass of drool on her shoulder, to feel her own throat's tender skin twisted in the heedless grip of a tiny hand, to brush her own face lightly against the plush-and-satin of the baby's cheek with its fierce bloom of hunger or its sleepy calm—this is not a typical rite of passage; it's extraordinary. To be reached for and called by name and prattled to in a toddling voice, to be able to give comfort with a gathering-up into her own thin girlish arms—this is a fantasy-privilege. A girl with a baby sibling is too young to bear the burdens and ambiguities of parenthood but old enough to know she's too young. And old enough to know that something impossible, something hopelessly sweet, has happened to her. In adulthood, it's no longer possible to fathom the magic of such a wish coming true. When it comes untrue…what then? Maybe the dreadful point of being caught by a butterfly is not in being caught, but in being left behind when it flies away.

In the afternoon sun, the butterfly has gone. This is all of summer: indoors, against a wall I sink to my knees, all the way down to the floor, my arms curving as if to cradle something that has been wrenched from me and thrust back, mutilated. My face twists, wracked. From my open mouth a droplet of drool falls and hits my arm as I dissolve into tears of intricate, almost-twenty-three-year-old pain, a pain whose dimensions I'm too old now to fully understand, and somehow still too young to bear.

\* \* \*

The greatest threat in having a beautiful thing is that it will one day disappear. The greatest danger of love is, of course, loss. Through our own death or theirs, we will lose every creature we'll ever love. But the terrible risk of cherishing something is rivaled only by the joy of cherishing it. Otherwise, no one would ever take such a terrible risk at all. Older-siblinghood may turn out to be the first experience of this choice, the choice to take the risk.

Long before your own children, before career, or maybe even before babysitting the neighbors' kids, there was your little brother or sister. To witness the daily development of a child, to take part in the nurturing when you yourself are still developing as a person, is a kind of ultimate privilege, because ordinarily this opportunity doesn't happen until parenthood.

You know their naptimes, their most precious toys, which cookies will kindle their eyes and which vegetables they'll invariably spit out, the games most likely to get them laughing, and the songs they like best at bedtime. You get the chance to teach them hundreds of important things, like how to use the word "actually" in a sentence, or how to jump rope or make a disgusting potion out of dish soap plus every condiment in the fridge, or how to sneak up on Dad with a water balloon, or how to button a shirt or imitate an elephant or breathe like Darth Vader or take care of a splinter or filch Jolly Ranchers before dinner without Mom finding out.

And while you're teaching them these indispensable things, what are they doing? First of all, they're egging you on. They love your outrageousness. They have no idea what "imagination" means, but they live it out with you every time you play make-believe, and there's no more natural sidekick, no more enthusiastic audience or eager co-conspirator, than a little kid—the wilder the ideas, the better. They follow you like a puppy; they want to be like you; they recognize you as one of them, a kid, someone who answers to the same authority but who knows the ropes far better than they do. They look to you for cues, they mimic your inflections, they learn your vocabulary, and they know for sure that you belong to them.

What they're really doing, unknowingly, is liberating you from the self-centered bubble of your own childhood. By nature of being so young, the little sibling is the first person who will ever love you *defenselessly*. For the first time in your life, you become the protector instead of the protected. They awaken in you an awareness of someone more vulnerable than yourself, someone you get to look out for. You don't have to, but if you choose to, you *get* to. And if life is such that the biological parents are physically or psychologically missing, you might in fact take on a substitute-parent role.

Because the character of sibling relationships is so individual, the possible variations are endless and defy simple definition. For an older sibling who looks after a younger one, the relationship is not parenthood and not same-age siblinghood but an amalgam with a nature all its own, the way purple is reddish and bluish... yet it's not redblue or bluered, but purple. Nothing else quite duplicates the mysterious alchemy of protectiveness and companionship, the strange echo that reverberates between someone poised at the beginning of childhood and someone poised at the end of it.

In just a few years, you're fellow adults. Your own little brother or sister pats you on the head, pours you some coffee and listens to your agonizing account of a breakup, teaches you how to download music, and then cracks up over a shared memory of childhood mayhem—*Remember how I wanted you to swing me around and you accidentally dislocated my elbow? Remember how you tore apart the sofa to build me a fort, and we both got in trouble?* Good things—graduations, shared gummy-snakes and glasses of lemonade. Bad things—bail, blood transfusions. But always there lingers the memory of someone smaller who literally looked up to you, and who knew safety and comfort in your arms or even your mere presence. One of their first words was your name.

And so it's an illusion that your heart breaks when a younger sibling dies, because in truth they break your heart the moment they arrive. The break holds itself together as long as they're here, but if you lose them, if they go, it's really just one tap on a chisel that's been poised for years. The pieces fall apart right along the original fracture, the one shaped uniquely like them…the one etched there from the day you first knew them. You were taking your first tentative steps toward adulthood, and taking its own literal first steps right next to you was this little creature, a charm, a sorcery, a pet and a playmate, imprinting itself with indelible tenderness on your own late-childhood years—those final vestiges of your own defenselessness. You don't know it's happening until it's already happened and already gone. Maybe that's why no one can explain how dangerous it is, and how incomparable, to be loved by a baby while still a child yourself.

\* \* \*

> *Come away, O human child!*
> *To the waters and the wild*
> *With a faery, hand in hand,*
> *For the world's more full of weeping than*
> *    you can understand.*

> —W. B. Yeats, "The Stolen Child"

# Lingering Thoughts
## on Salvage

W hen we aren't in tears or in a stupor of grief, or numbed in some escapist activity, there are times when we're quiet, blinking like nap-dazed children, looking around, surveying. We're trying to figure out where we are, and what will become of us. Over and over again we have to learn that we can't find our lost one no matter what we do, where we look, how hard we try, how long we search, or even how staunchly we refuse to give up.

There's no guide to living this way. To stop hurting is not the important thing. Now is not the time for that. Now is for learning how to breathe *within* a pain we can't describe and couldn't prepare for even if we knew it was coming.

In confusion and protest, we start practicing because we have no choice. We rehearse living with situations we never intended or wanted to live with. It goes against nature. Our insides are in a shambles.

If griefwork is learning to balance the weight of loss so we can move beneath it, and keep living without stumbling and swaying and falling every few steps, then we're like toddlers learning to walk. We crash repeatedly.

We could avoid the worst of it if we were placed in a walker or tied to a chair, or carried or hand-held by others, or drugged on painkillers and pushed out the door. But we won't learn, then. If we're ever to learn to walk steadily on our own, we can't avoid the necessary injuries.

# Discovery

## Chapter 20

# Us and Them

(Isolation From the Nonbereaved)

In the first few months, there are many tokens of sympathy from other people. A bouquet, or a little cactus, a basket of ferns and ivy, every last one of the greeting cards—each one is important. But eventually the cards stop appearing, the phone calls come less frequently, and some people seem to fade away altogether. Mike observes pithily, "Everybody else gets over your grief a lot faster than you do."

I go to work and come home. Sometimes when my car is in for repairs, I borrow my little brother's car. At the hands of my mom, it's been festooned with more rosaries, holy cards, stuffed animals, bumper stickers, and general kitschy paraphernalia than a parish country fair, but I don't care. I like having something of his close to me at work. Too often now, my mind congeals into a pulseless blob before the workday is over, and my eyes feel as dull as two scuffed marbles that have lost the poise of alertness and rolled to the side of an empty dish.

My performance rating at work reflects this state of preoccupation. It's an inferior rating, but it's realistic. The paperwork indicates that my accomplishments were made "despite difficult personal circumstances" and goes on to enumerate those tasks that I'd completed, although I forgot them even as I did them. When I review the form, my attention snags on one word. I make no objection to the performance rating itself, but I request that the wording of it be changed and the paperwork be redone. The so-called personal circumstance, an empty and meaningless phrase, needed to be called by its name (and its name is not "Difficult"). The revision matters to no one besides me, but that's OK.

Socially, I'm not yet back to the usual round of activities. I tell a man I've recently met that I'm not ready to return to the dating scene. This man puts it all neatly into perspective for me. "Sorry to hear about your brother," he writes in an email, "but that's life—people die." This statement is inarguably true but so ghoulishly ill-timed that I stare at the email, marveling at its insensitivity.

I understand: it's not cruelty; it's simply people being people, doing what they can to avoid pain. Usually I'm one of the "other people" too—I'll attend a funeral out of respect for someone else's loss, and for a while I'm sad, but it's with some relief that I soon turn back to my own daily cares, grateful to be drawn back into the steadiness of normal routine. No one wants to think too clearly or too often about death, and right now, to see me is to experience a reminder, a jolt of fear. What's happened to me gives others a glimmer of what might be in store for them. I can't blame them for not wanting to be reminded. It's unsettling to know that my very presence tolls like the proverbial bell.

Yet there are people who brave the jolt of fear, people who don't let it stop them from offering kindness. Among the many sympathy cards that arrive in the weeks after the crash, I receive one from a colleague, Katy. We weren't particularly close friends, but to my surprise the next few months are punctuated by more cards from her, sometimes accompanied by a book, always with a simple question: "How are you doing?" Many times over, I read and reread these unexpected greetings, stunned by their sensitivity.

* * *

The primary separation—from our lost person—is obvious, and now the secondary separations are showing more clearly every day. We may become a little quieter when we're out in the world. Idle conversation seems pointless, an irritating distraction. Don't people realize what's really important? If they did, surely they'd stop chattering about inconsequential things? But they continue on as before, leaving us behind. We're as separate from other people, the world of general indifference, as if we were in another cosmos.

This indifference isn't a bad thing. Without it, we humans would have foundered in our first generation of grief. The world's life goes on, no matter who's in it and who isn't, but the newly bereaved are a walking, breathing, distressingly clear sign that there are no guarantees about loss. It's lonely, feeling like an example, a dire warning. To others, our grief must be like a glacial wind slicing down from a mountain, a wind with a whisper: *This time, it's happening to them...next time it could be you, and then it will be you with the desolate eyes, you unable to eat, you whose guts are knotted so tightly that you can't breathe, you who weeps piteously day after sodden day and night after night after long pallid night, knowing how useless it is but unable to stop, because you're driven by pain that gets all its power from how much you love the person you've lost.*

Most often we're among the generic "others," outsiders whose lives aren't truly disrupted except for a passing wave of sympathy. We can feel awful for someone in a bad situation, but we aren't in it ourselves—and we don't want to be. Our boat may rock a little bit, but it doesn't tip over. We feel our deck pitch off balance, but we quickly regain our equilibrium and go on.

When it's our very own boat that capsizes and tips us into the icy fathoms, some brave, patient others will jump in for a while with us, but one by one they will climb out, back into their own boats, because (1) they can, and (2) they must. It's difficult not to take this personally, but it isn't personal. It is only human nature. "Us and them" is only an artificial separation, after all—for the moment, "they" are simply the ones who were lucky this time. And among them we discover, at random, that there are some who've fallen in before us and still remember the cold, and the vastness of being alone in it. One day, maybe soon, we'll find ourselves reaching our own hand across the freezing depths to help someone else.

## CHAPTER 21

# The Feverbreak of Autumn

(Isolation Among Family)

August. The summer ripens bitterly, a blighted fruit. By September, routines reassert themselves, including the routines of how family members interact.

Back in May, we'd been stunned out of our characteristic behavior. During the funeral Mass, my dad delivered a self-effacing eulogy that inadvertently highlighted the tree from which the (likewise spectacularly gifted but modest) apple had not fallen far, but that's not what was out of character. When he was finished and the priest had resumed the service, my father stood up and cut politely but definitely into the prayers, to ask that Tim, Mike, Matt, and I also be given a chance to speak. (The idea of my dad interrupting a priest in the middle of a service, in a huge church? Unheard of.) I'd read aloud the poem I'd written the night before (I generally never read things aloud in public, least of all my own home-baked verse), and Tim took my arm as we walked back to our seats. (None of us ever takes anyone else's arm.) I recalled Mike helping me to stay on my feet, in the funeral home. (The gesture itself and the need for it were both completely alien.) None of this behavior was remotely like ourselves, but the circumstances were extraordinary.

After a few months, though, each of us has started to fit the loss into our own distinct lives. We were leveled to the ground together, but we have not *become* each other. Inevitably, individual communication styles remain true. The openly verbal stay that way; the typically reticent are quiet. Among my brothers and me, the subject of the loss comes up only when necessary; we mention our brother in reminiscence when the conversation calls for it, but the conversation is never deliberately taken into the territory of his death unless there is a specific reason to do so.

Some of us are of a religious or spiritual leaning; others are not. "Your brother is at peace now in heaven," many people say. Not being religious, I'm not sure how to reply, but eventually I realize I don't have to. The thought and the intention are enough.

I go to Ocean City in New Jersey with my parents for a weekend. That afternoon on the boardwalk, the atmosphere between them is distraught; they argue; they walk apart. When evening comes, the three of us sit on a balcony as the moon rises. My parents have made up, in their fashion, by allowing the disagreement to lapse until finally it's nothing more than a few token contradictions, which dwindle still further into listless remarks. I wait through their lingering conversation until it is full dark, the sea awash with moonlight. Their talk ceases, and at length the silence on the balcony is engulfed by the susurrations of the surf. Shushed at last, we watch the waves, all three of us facing outward from our separate chairs on the tiny balcony.

Summer gives way to autumn.

\* \* \*

There are still more losses to be faced. Even within the smallest communities of grief, even among those whose pain is as intense as ours, ultimately we need to manage on our own. In the cauldron of shared pain, we mix for a time, but we don't dissolve. We're each a self, and sooner or later must tend the self's pain alone.

Styles of expression may differ. The verbal person seeks engagement, to take refuge in an exchange: *Why can't we talk about it? Isn't it a thousand times more painful, to not talk about it?* In stark contrast, the reticent person seeks refuge in solitude, not wanting to be pursued or accused of shutting others out: *Must we keep talking about it? Isn't it clear that sometimes communication simply hurts too much?*

When it comes to beliefs, it's not that they *may* differ. Beliefs *will* differ. It's the hot button of hot buttons: spirituality. God, afterlife, faith, belief, is-this-the-end-or-only-the-beginning… the issues over which we can disagree are endless. And people may be uncomfortable with a lack of any definitive stand: surely one must believe *something?* Some people are passionately sure there's more to existence than this world, and it's painful for them to witness others struggling with what seems like unnecessary doubt: *How hard it must be to get up in the morning, let alone carry on in the face of loss, if you don't believe in an afterlife? Why would you turn away from the comfort of it?* But for others, uncertainty is the only thing they're sure of: *None of us knows these things for sure; doubt is part of human life. Why deny the human condition?*

When we don't happen to share the certainties of those nearby, we may end up feeling like spiritual porcupines, as if our particular ideas are unseemly quills, offensive or pitiable to those around us who think differently. Or worse, we may feel as if someone is trying to pull our quills out or flatten them down, to coax us into agreement, or we may try to coax someone else into agreement with us. But this means that the need to ratify our beliefs, or the need for connection and reassurance, is getting in the way of our respect for who that other person is. There are times when the only harmony we can have is that which comes from accepting disharmony.

We muddle through inadvertent cruelties, our own and other people's. Sometimes another's gates are closed, no matter how much we don't like it, and sometimes we need to close our own gates, even if we wish it could be otherwise. Much of the time, none of us really knows what to do.

## Chapter 22

# Are and Were and Was and Is

(How Much to Reveal or Explain, or Not)

*We are seven.*

—William Wordsworth, "We Are Seven"

There are many practical considerations. I've taken care of many details, such as recording his voicemail message on my laptop, and buying a fireproof box to store the tiny lock of his hair, a bit of dirt and glass from the crash scene, and certain photos for which I don't have negatives and which are therefore irreplaceable. But in spite of my diligence, small, unexpected problems appear.

There is the matter of how to inform a casual questioner about the size of my family of origin. "Do you have any brothers and sisters?" is such a common question in everyday conversation that I need to prepare for it quickly. I consider whether I *have* four brothers, or I *had* four brothers. It's an important distinction, fraught with issues of privacy and accuracy: saying I "had four" sounds like I did at one time but don't anymore, which requires me to explain something I may not want to explain. Saying I "have three" brothers is illogical too, as if one of them never existed. But continuing to say that I "have four" fails to acknowledge something pivotal. What, then, to say?

I find myself answering differently, depending on who's asking. In casual conversation with a stranger who asks how many brothers and sisters I have, I answer simply: four. If someone asks me about them, I clarify: four brothers; three living and one who is deceased. It's true and easy to say, once I get used to it. The word "deceased" is greeting-card formal, not requiring acknowledgment and in fact slightly discouraging it. It lets the casual questioner know that there need be no awkward pause, there will be no sudden upwelling of emotion like a snake unexpectedly crawling out of my handbag, from which the observer must jump back hastily; it can be taken as it is, a flat fact, and dismissed. It also indicates politely that I don't want to discuss things in detail, a sort of conversational rope swing to get me from one place to another without bogging down in the quicksand of something too personal. "Deceased" is socially acceptable, its real meaning soothingly neutralized. It's almost like saying, "Three in the suburbs and one who lives in the city."

More rarely, I'll make a subtle revision: "Three living and one who died." That tiny change allows further interest or even an expression of sympathy. The word "died" is so much more vulnerable—as a culture we tiptoe around it with an array of euphemisms like "passed away" and "passed on" and "deceased" and "crossed over" and "no longer with us." "Died" is blunt. "Killed" is even more startling. I don't use these words except in very rare cases; they're only for sharing one of my most carefully kept secrets: not just the fact that he existed, but also how we lost him, and what he means. The details of him are what I guard from the general public indifference. Somehow I owe him this protection—he's still my little brother.

\* \* \*

In the poem "We Are Seven" by William Wordsworth, the narrator meets a little girl and asks how large her family is. She explains that she has six brothers and sisters, and therefore they are "seven in all." Upon further questioning, however, it comes to light that one brother and one sister are dead. Apparently wanting her to account for this in the final tally of family members, the narrator repeats his question as if he were a schoolmaster gently prompting her for the correct answer:

*"How many are you, then," said I,*
*"If they two are in heaven?"*
*Quick was the little Maid's reply,*
*"O Master! We are seven."*

A disagreement ensues. It's unclear why the matter should be worth such persistence to the narrator, but evidently it is. Finally, in the last stanza of the poem, the winner of the debate emerges:

*"But* [the narrator protests] *they are dead; those two are dead!*
*Their spirits are in heaven!"*
*'Twas throwing words away; for still*
*The little Maid would have her will,*
*And said, "Nay, we are seven!"*

The little dickens is in denial, the narrator seems to imply, but one can't help admiring her conviction.

Sometimes we defend the rightful place of our lost person, sharing certain information as a way of preserving their memory. In other instances, we might decide to keep certain things to ourselves, certain emotions and certain facts. People may say "Don't be ashamed," but it's not shame; it's privacy. It's a refusal to expose the particular, the sanctified personal things. Keeping some information private is simply a different way of guarding our loved one's memory. For the outside world, we can use *was*, but in the heart, *is* will always be *is*.

## CHAPTER 23

# Faultlines

(Cause, Effect, and Responsibility)

When I'm not dealing with practical concerns like how to tell people (or not tell them) things, there are intellectual things to ponder too. The events that led to this death were not uncomplicated. Although it was just one car, it was a drunk-driving crash. A review of the facts produces reactions that skid up and down like the needle of a seismograph:

*He didn't have to go out that night, but he did. He wanted to—it was meant to be a night of fun with two friends. He bought them flowers; he bought them drinks.* If they'd done something at one of their homes, then the whole thing would never…?

*He wasn't wearing a seatbelt.* If he'd been more aware, more coherent, he might have buckled himself in and then maybe he'd have had a chance of surviving…?

*He wasn't driving; he was in the backseat. But the other girls were drunk too. No designated driver.* I'm nonreligious, but Holy Jesus Christ. If they'd considered that one single precaution, then almost certainly it would never have happened…?

*On the drive home, they turned around so they could try to rescue a deer they'd passed, and possibly run over, on the highway. He'd wanted to call the police.* Perhaps if they hadn't stopped, or if they'd called the police, then maybe…?

*After they pulled the deer to the roadside, debated calling the police, and continued on their way, the two inebriated young women in the front seat started fighting, all control was lost, and then Dave was lost.* Foolish, all of them. In the course of that evening, did any of them ever sense the gathering momentum of disaster? (In the course of his entire life, did any of us?)

\* \* \*

How do events line up so inexorably, each one a potential stopping point but somehow hurtling on unchecked, until, in an instant, they become something so singular and irretrievable? We need to know not just what happened—when, where, how they died—but also *why*. Whose fault was the death? Why did the person do whatever he or she did? Why didn't he or she [fill in here any number of alternatives]?

One of the purposes of figuring out the cause is to assign responsibility. Was it a true accident, could it have been averted; was it something willful like a murder or a suicide? And if responsibility belongs to someone still living, have they compensated? We ask ourselves whether the dead deserved to die, whether the survivors deserve the pain of the loss. If being in this pain means somehow we deserve it, then...what for? We beg to know: what have we done to deserve this?

We place a premium on intent. Our outrage on behalf of someone who has been killed, and our leniency toward any culpable person, come largely from what we think they *meant to do*. If our loved one was murdered or died in an accident that they couldn't have prevented, we feel one way; if they died deliberately by their own hand, we feel another way; if they died trying to hurt someone else, we feel still another way, and yet another if they died due to their own poor judgment.

The anger at having been suddenly denied this person's presence may in fact belong to that person. If the lost one played a part in his or her own death, of course we'll be upset with them. Just because they aren't here to receive our reaction doesn't mean we have no reaction. But if the person is not here, where can any of our reactions go? We desperately want to tell the person what we feel about all this, ask them to tell us their side of the story (*Why did you do that?*), and give them a reprieve (*Everyone makes mistakes—just please don't do it again.*). Or maybe they made no mistake at all, and were instead the victim of an illness or sudden violence from someone else. We desperately want to tell them: *You didn't deserve this.* And if they died trying to hurt someone else, we agonize: *How, why, did it come to this?*

The one answer we will not accept is that "it doesn't matter because the person is already dead." It *does* matter. Maybe at least the thing can be prevented from happening to someone else. If we have to accept the death, at least we can try to learn something from it, even if the beneficiaries of that knowledge are people we'll never meet. We can't recoup our loss; we can only— maybe—save someone else from a similar fate.

## CHAPTER 24

# This Time

(Inadequacy, Failure, and Regret)

My mother has told me of the final evening, when Dave was at home for a little while. He and my parents had been to Moravian that morning to view his exhibits in the senior art show, and in the evening after they'd all returned to my parents' house, Dave had been looking around for a snack. There were pears in the fridge; he grabbed one, but my mom remembered there was another that already had a sliver cut from it, and she suggested he might as well finish that one first. Obligingly, he'd eaten the cut-into pear, gone on his way, and the evening ended with the police at my parents' door.

She tells me later: she wishes she'd just let him have a whole, uncut pear, instead of bothering about being efficient and finishing up the cut-into pear first. He shouldn't, she feels, have had to make do with part of a pear when there were whole ones available. He'd been the fifth child, always having to make do; he should have been able to enjoy a whole pear.

Of course it wasn't about the pear, really—if he'd wanted more, he would have asked for more, because there were plenty of pears. It was really about wanting to give more than just enough, wanting to stop worrying about being practical and simply bestow. To give profligately, to lavish. And there's no clearer symbol of nourishment and nurturing and the giving of abundance, than food.

We give and receive gifts of food, we use it to satisfy emotional needs and to perform social rituals; we use it as a second language, a way to reach each other. Even rejecting an offer of food can be done in a variety of ways, to offend or appease, to deter or encourage, as if the food were a surrogate for the person offering it.

Dave, always a spare eater, could deliver an exquisitely *accepting* rejection. When asked if he wanted a portion and he didn't, his answer was never a simple "No." It was some variety of "Not really" or "Not right now," which frequently led to a refrigerator crammed with leftovers of all sorts, from a sandwich with only a few bites taken out of it, to an eighth of a McDonald's chocolate shake in its soggy, wax-flecked paper cup. My own fridge has always overflowed with such remnants; I'm entirely in sympathy with the philosophy of never throwing leftovers away, no matter how sparse and pathetic the portion might be, because one will almost certainly want it later. Leftovers represent the difference between No and Eventually-yes.

I speak in this language myself. In my own last phone conversation with Dave, which had been brief and prosaic, he asked if I was coming to our parents' house for dinner that day, and I'd said, "I can't this time." But I'd recently shown him a pencil portrait I'd drawn of him as a baby, and I told him I'd get it framed and bring it back to him as soon as possible. "OK," he said, "cool."

The words of the conversation appeared to reveal almost nothing; the important information was entirely implied: "this time" is only a temporary situation; there will be a next time. I'm not saying No; I'm only saying Not-quite-yet. He's not saying Forget it; he's saying OK, I'll wait for you. Like semaphores at night, these signals——you have to be alert even to detect them, let alone read their meanings. But for those who speak the language, there's nothing more accommodating than "Cool" and nothing more reassuring than "Not this time."

But not this time. And with that, I come to the heart of things. Should have done something; should have been there. These are not the if-only's about his behavior; these are the if-only's that belong to the self alone: *I might have prevented it, if only I'd... or if only I hadn't...!* But I didn't do whatever that thing might have been; I did something else instead, and look what happened.

As toddlers at play, Matt and Dave would reach up and scream "Pre-tect me!" to one of us older kids when another was pretending to chase after him. Prevent; protect. Always, we did; always the protector came through, swung the little kid up into the arms of safety. But not this time. Maybe I couldn't have, even if I'd had the chance. How many opportunities were there, on that night or any other time, between each of us and him, in which one or another of us might have done something differently and prevented the whole thing? I understand my mother's fixation with the uncut pear: even if we couldn't have stopped the events unfolding how they did, how many chances were there to lavish, one last time?

Whatever life was at that moment, whatever any of us did or were or gave or hoped or promised, it was inadequate to keep him here. And maybe it was inadequate to convey what we'd have wanted him to know: *An entire pear, a bushel, a cornucopia, harvests upon harvests of pears or pre-tecting or a moment more of my attention or anything else you wish for...this time, any time, every time.*

\* \* \*

We're closing in on what matters most. Inconsequential things are now laden with meaning and they're tolling in our memory: Absence. A rejection. Distance, alienation. A snarl, an insult, a fight, a coldness. The word "no." And whatever we did give, it wasn't just lacking in lavishness—it wasn't even sufficient to save the person's life. Sometimes that conclusion is based on an illusion of a power we didn't really have. Other times, it reflects the most human of all demons: failure.

There are many failures to account for. A prayer in the Catholic Mass called the Confiteor sums it up: *what I have done, and what I have failed to do.* There is everything from the distant past, to how things transpired the last time we interacted with the lost person. Maybe we missed a chance to see them; maybe we fought, said mean things, flung off in a huff, hung up on them, or never called them in the first place.

We might try to get back to that moment—that last time we interacted with them and didn't do whatever might have "saved" them—to remember what our reasons and motivations were, so we can scrutinize those motivations for selfishness, laziness, or any potential legitimacy. Maybe the person got on our nerves, said something annoying to us, betrayed our trust, or ignored us… or maybe we're just jerks, maybe we lacked character, maybe we weren't a good enough sister, brother, parent, friend. Maybe we sense we've failed on a grand scale, or at a pivotal moment somewhere in the past, but we haven't figured out exactly how or when or why. Or maybe we figured it out, but too late. At the final moment, we failed to prevent the death. Maybe even, however inadvertently, we contributed to it somehow.

This is intolerably painful if the lost person was younger and once trusted in our protection. When a dear friend or relative or partner is threatened, we go into Protective Mode, possibly at the risk of our lives, but in ordinary day-to-day living, we don't think of them as needing protection; they're capable of surviving just fine on their own. But if the threat is to someone we care about who's younger than we are, our sense of responsibility is on a higher setting. Actual age doesn't matter; we might both be elderly or we might both be kids, and the other person might be physically much bigger and hardier in every way. By now they may even have developed a sense of protectiveness toward us. But despite all that, if we've known them since they were vulnerable to every kind of harm, if we've always responded when we heard the call, "Pre-tect me," then our failure this time feels like our most grievous failure of all. It doesn't matter if it was technically in our power or not. It doesn't matter if we're not thinking rationally. At the simplest level we see the situation: we didn't protect them.

How should we judge ourselves then, harshly or with leniency? Because there's no point pretending that we won't judge ourselves. This kind of judgment doesn't help matters, but we sometimes feel compelled to do it anyway, so we may as well get it out in the open.

It might have been entirely out of our hands, and the unfairness of that will weigh on us for the rest of our lives. Or it may be the case that if we'd done something differently, the death might not have happened. Sometimes an innocent oversight, or tiredness, or a lapse in vigilance, or even something as sordid as a petty fight, may turn out to have been a contributing factor or even a deciding factor in whether someone lived or died. Human failings, innocent mistakes, minor limitations, can lead to catastrophe completely at odds with our intentions, and now it's too late to take anything back.

It can be very painful to acknowledge this, and others might try to discourage us from what appears to be pointless guilt because they don't want to see us "beat ourselves up." But it's also possible that others see something more clearly than we do. They see that even if our action led directly to the person's death, that doesn't mean we wanted the death to happen. It comes back to intent, directed at ourselves this time. If a plate falls to the floor because we flung it down in anger or because we knocked it off a shelf by accident, the result is the same: it shatters. Natural laws like gravity and momentum are inevitable; the outcome is the same no matter how it comes about. In that way, nature has no bias, and no mercy. Human nature, on the other hand, does. It understands the intangible difference between action and intention.

Self-acceptance is elusive. We may feel we're indulging in selfish weakness, or betraying our loved one, if we allow our sense of failure to diminish like an untended fire. The philosophy of penance is voluntary house arrest, keeping the scales of justice balanced to make up for wrong deeds and neglected opportunities, but mea culpa can be carried too far. How do we know when we've gone too far? How do we finally recognize that the sound of a gavel banging in judgment is actually preventing us from real understanding?

The answer may have nothing to do with whether we "ought to" forgive ourselves. The answer may be in the fact that the situation is about more than just ourselves and our regret. There is someone else involved here, someone who cannot speak for themselves but who deserves a voice.

*Would they believe us if we said we were sorry?* Would the lost person forgive our failures, even ones that ended like this? If we've known that person at any depth, we already know the answer.

*If the situation were reversed, would they have asked our forgiveness for wrong words or wrong deeds, and would we grant it?* Part of us wishes a lifetime of this doubt upon them, instead of the other way around, because at least that way they'd be getting a lifetime. Would we want them to presume upon our mercy? Yes.

Even if it doesn't change what happened, can we then accept a presumed mercy from them, knowing they'd be hurt if we didn't accept it? Would we reject what we know would be their compassion for us, if they could only speak it?

To dismiss these answers just because we can't hear the person say the words, is to dismiss the person's character simply because they're not here. We know what the person would say to us if they could. Acknowledging it is one of the ways we respect their essential selfhood. If we know in truth that they'd want us to presume upon *their* mercy, then to accept it is a gesture of humility toward them, toward what we know about their character. It's also one of the first ways we learn to go on living with them even after they've died.

## CHAPTER 25

# Silent Night

(Holidays)

In December, as the end of the month approaches, I tell my mother that I can't come to the family dinner on Christmas Day. *Can't* is precisely the right word. I cannot do it. I can think only of how my chair at the dinner table was next to Dave's, and how this year I won't be able to bear up, not even for the sake of others. I set aside my gifts for later.

In my living room, Christmas passes like an ordinary winter day. The only seasonal decoration I have on display is an ornament, called a Partridge in a Pear, which I bought one summer and loved so much that I've always kept it on display year-round anyway. It's a small ceramic pear (of all things) of pale greenish gold and rose, with a matte glaze finish. Its top and bottom halves are connected with a tiny hinge, so that the pear opens like an egg to reveal a tiny glass partridge with gold-tipped wings nestling inside. The partridge has a loop of golden thread attached to its top so it can be taken out and hung as an ornament on a Christmas tree, but my favorite way to display it has always been with the partridge suspended from the top half of the pear itself, as if the bird were hovering just within the fruit, sheltered but unconfined.

This year, what I see is a little bird in a pear the color of nature's first green-and-gold. The symbolism is accidental and

131

absurd and entirely too heavy. After this year, I'll be able to participate in holidays, but in my own life's calendar, Christmas 2004 is only my little bird and an empty silent night.

* * *

We come up suddenly against our own limits. As mysterious as we may seem to others, whose own limits are different, we might find that there are specific things we simply can't do the same way now that we've lost a certain person. This might be temporary or it might be permanent—we have no way of knowing whether we'll one day be able to do these things again, or whether we'll even want to. For now, we have to make a different plan, and invent a different way.

## CHAPTER 26

# Down the Stairs

(The Worst Things)

For most of a week the following spring, we go as a family to a local county courthouse where the woman who had been driving the car is tried for vehicular manslaughter. On the first day, the family gathers in the parking lot. When Matt arrives, I reach up to hug him, shocked as always at how tall he is, and the only thing I can think of to say—foolishly, pointlessly—is, "My bébé." I'm not sure if he even hears it, but he's always been as unswervingly tolerant as Dave of my occasional lapses into sentiment. He accepts this one by simply hugging me back without saying anything, a kindness I never forget.

For several days the trial becomes our temporary job and the family waiting area our office. The court hall has vending machines, restrooms, and local little restaurants where we can get something to eat at lunchtime. In the afternoons, we reassemble for the second shift of Observing the Proceedings.

At times, I'm suspended, listening to the trial but also carried away in my own mind, because the outcome of the trial pales in comparison to certain other questions that no judge or jury will ever be able to answer. I was given the autopsy report to read in the detective's office, and now I think about the details of it, along with the information the investigating officers have gathered in the past nine months, about exactly how and why the crash was fatal. Fractured skull, shattered facial bones, crushed lungs. My parents have asked me, "Do you think he died instantly?" "Yes," I've said, my heart sick with hope—*hope?*—that the violence was too extreme and too quick, that there wasn't time for pain. We've even tried to take desperate comfort in the possibility that maybe he'd been asleep in the backseat.

In the courtroom, events are recounted meticulously. As the woman on trial gives her testimony, she describes a struggle for the steering wheel between herself and the other woman in the front seat, with them screaming at each other and Dave screaming at both of them to stop. (Not asleep, then.) The prosecutor replays the 911 call a passing driver made in the seconds after the crash occurred. The voice is that of a young man—he is in court today—who surely never imagined he'd be the narrator of such a scene: the car ahead of him speeding, veering and swerving, catching on the edge of the roadside ditch and somersaulting, and finally, at last, the endless tumble coming to an eerie finish, the headlights still on but pointing in the wrong direction and someone on the ground, motionless. The dispatcher's voice tries to give instructions, but the young caller's voice rises, goes frantic. "Oh my God," he cries, as if the dispatcher is failing to appreciate the most important point. "The kid in the ditch—*what about the fucking kid?*"

It is clear to everyone in the courtroom whom he is referring to. Everyone can envision the scene, and so that no detail might be missed, the jury is shown enlarged photos of it. The placards are kept carefully turned away from us, to spare us the graphic details, or perhaps simply to minimize our reaction in front of the jury. And now the judge, in a quiet but still-audible voice, describes the photographs with journalistic clarity for the stenographer to record. As he murmurs his summaries, I hear the word "face-down." I'm suddenly very aware of my mother, as if she's spoken to me, but she hasn't said a word and we aren't even looking at each other. Some last-remaining endurance within me that has been strained to its limit is finally wrenched too far, and it breaks just then. I never speak of it. (Later, again and again, with my hands clenched around my head and pulling at my own hair, I'll rock back and forth and cling to the only thing left: *The soft grass, at least; not the pavement, not the pavement, not the pavement...*)

After the trial ends, we go to the detective's office on the second floor of the police station to retrieve Dave's so-called last effects, which have been kept as evidence and consist only of the clothes he wore that night. While my parents are in another room asking courteously after a junior officer who has been bitten by a dog, the detective hands me a paper bag that contains Dave's things. I reach out and enfold it in my arms, tuck it against my side in the same way Tim and Mike and I used to carry the bébés downstairs and upstairs and through the house, the supermarket, the park, or wherever, innumerable other times a long time ago. That gesture of carting around a little kid, how deeply ingrained it is (hoisting him up, settling him against your hip, and hanging on casually as you walk along, while he examines a toy in his hands, instinctively leaning his own weight out just far enough to achieve a perfect cantilevered balance). I start down the stairs.

As I take each step, bits of the trial come into my head. I envision the paramedics arriving at the crash scene with what must, I imagine, be an all-too-familiar recognition of the mess. I envision them quickly dismissing Dave because he can't be saved, and busying themselves with the two women, one of whom is quite shaken, the other suffering a broken foot. When time permitted, the paramedics would then have picked up my brother's body and put it in a heavy plastic bag, and bundled it into an ambulance. Unceremonious. Thinking about it, you try not to take it personally, the detachment, the efficiency; it's the way of the world, the final consignment. We're none of us exempt. Still, you can feel the entreaty in yourself: *Please be careful, I know he means nothing to you, but*...I remember a liturgical music class in Catholic elementary school, when I learned a song that depicted the perspective of Mary, the mother of Jesus, pleading with the soldiers who handled her son before and after the crucifixion. "Carry Him Gently," the song was called. Because what else can be done except to treat what remains with deference?

My thoughts wander farther back to earlier elementary school, to *The Illustrated Book of the Saints* that I'd read in second grade. Each saint's story was summarized in a few paragraphs and illustrated in lively colors. There were martyrs holding lambs or lilies or crucifixes, saints radiating virtue or undergoing mysterious sanctification, missionaries sharing their worldly goods with the poor or protecting the helpless. Those lives of the most extreme holiness often involved a certain amount of violence, and with the unerring fascination of childhood, I knew exactly which pictures showed crimson droplets trickling decorously but vividly from foreheads or the palms of martyred hands. Among these images, the picture of St. Sebastian was the most troubling, and inspired the most anxious pity: his wrists tied to a tree, he is in the very process of being impaled by a flurry of arrows; his eyes are wide and he's gasping as his lungs are speared, impossibly and multiply speared, blood oozing beneath the arrows that have already punctured that pale defenseless chest. Unlike the other pictures of the humbly glorified, for whom the mechanics of martyrdom have already been accomplished, this picture is graphic and inescapable. The moment of agony, frozen: St. Sebastian condemned not to be dead, but to be *dying*, forever.

I reach the bottom of the staircase, set the bag down on a chair, and open it. Inside are my brother's clothes and his brown leather shoes. The police have told us that they'd found one shoe in the grass, away from him. The thought of the shoe, torn from him that way, pierces me. There are specific tears that belong to this detail alone, that I will cry later, many times. It's easy to say that the whole thing may have been "over so quickly," but in some dark well of my mind, time has frozen at that moment, a moment that never ends: the moment in which my little brother is condemned not to be dead, but to be *dying*, forever.

I pick up the bag again. Its haunting lightness somehow conveys the economy of an entire existence. Dave had occupied his clothes unobtrusively, hidden in them always with plenty of left-over space, so they hung loosely, barely suggesting the body within. His spare physique, tall and narrow and pale as St. Sebastian...and there was the way he walked, loping yet collected to himself, as if politely declining his legitimate allotment of space. The energy of his life was in other things: in the staggering artistry of a mind that refracted moods and ideas and then cast them in restless carnivals of color; in the indiscriminate, adventuresome kindness like a tollbooth light stuck heedlessly and good-naturedly on green; in the scheme-inclined humor always simmering, along with the interior uncertain sadness of a nocturnal soul; even in the wildly curly hair that he often tucked completely beneath a beanie he'd bought at a thrift shop.

I wish his final journey hadn't been managed by indifferent, weary strangers. There's only one thing we can do about that now. Here at the police station, I carry the bag outside with both my arms around it; I bring it to my mother and she reaches out to receive it in a manner extremely familiar. It's another ritual we shouldn't have to devise, but which is necessary now. We're bringing the lone paper bag safely home to rest, in just one more among all the other gestures of honor and affection for the kid in the ditch—for David, whose name means "beloved."

\* \* \*

The lowest depth to which we descend is no longer anything about us, or guilt or regret for our failings, or even our loss. The most difficult layer of grief is the depth at which we're most helpless and for which there is no comfort. It's about what matters most: the person younger than we, who suffered their pain and died their death without us.

Others, in their compassion, see some of our darker thoughts as needless, self-inflicted pain, and they can hardly bear to see us driven to such a state of morbid horror, apparently to no purpose.

*Don't torture yourself.*

*It's over now.*

*There's nothing you could have done; there's no point in tor-menting yourself.*

*Stop doing this to yourself—*

*—let it go—*

*—it's already over for him—*

*—it won't help her now—*

*—thinking about it won't bring them back...*

Of course it won't—we're very aware of that. All the euphemisms, the grace notes, the careful discreetness—these things do distract us, but we always know exactly what we're being distracted *from*. We've already been down to those depths, and even if we never show it, we'll go there countless more times in our secret heart. Why?

We still care, and care is the guardian of the things we most desperately don't want to acknowledge but that we know are true—the terrible things, and the too-lateness of succor or amends. How could we *not* think about these things? The only way to bear them is to not avoid them. We need to be there at the moment of our loved one's death, even if only in thought.

The need to face the worst, to endure the horrible things vicariously, is both a literal act and a powerful symbol of our thwarted devotion. Our loved one doesn't "need" our protection or attention anymore, but the love itself is still very much alive, and maybe it does need these things. Like pride, affection survives its own object. It's living within us, it still feels pain, and, perhaps most fantastically, still responds to nurture even though its object will never return.

There are things we would change, if only we could. There are things we want to do and things we want to have, even though we can't. There are things the person suffered, and we couldn't prevent them. We can't undo these things, not with a lifetime of pleas to God or anyone. There's nothing that can ever wipe these knowings out—and if we try to ignore or minimize them, we're hounded by this self-deception for the rest of our lives. If our awareness of the most painful details is blunted too often, or we find ourselves being hushed "for our own good," we may clutch all the harder and become obsessed.

The idea that our loved person died alone, in pain, sick, confused, lost, freezing, drowning, burning, choking, bleeding, tormented, in tears, terror, squalor, rage, or self-hatred, struggling for the breath to call out, wishing for help or a few more minutes of life or the comfort of a familiar face, but all in vain—these ideas can never be soothed away. These thoughts aren't necessarily for every day, and maybe they aren't meant to become the guiding force of our own life, but certain things really happened to a person incalculably precious to us, and sometimes the truest thing we can do is to stop avoiding and instead articulate our knowledge, in whatever way we can.

At the same time, the things we know or suspect or imagine about the last moments of our loved one's life are so painful that they must be endured in fragments or they can't be endured at all. Even the mind hesitates to face them, and guards them with its own gaze mostly averted. Our attention approaches only in solitary flickers, because these intuitions are wounds of the most savage tenderness. The darkest things are kept in a deep and quiet inner sanctum, but they *are* kept. What we need is to be allowed, and to allow ourselves, to carry them gently.

## CHAPTER 27

# Dennis and Virginia

### (The Simplest Wish)

*B*ut a Samaritan, as he traveled, came where the man was; and when
he saw him, he took pity on him. He went to him and bandaged
his wounds, pouring on oil and wine. Then he put the man on his own
donkey, brought him to an inn and took care of him. (Luke 10:34–35)

### 1. Dennis

It's 2005. I'm in the car with a boyfriend; we're on Route
202, passing through a town. He suddenly looks to the right and
asks, "Is that guy dead? Should we stop?" At first I have no idea
what he means, and only as we pass the roadside scene do I see: a
man in shorts and a T-shirt is lying all wrong and upside down in
the grass beside the road, amid a hapless group of passersby. We
pull over and dash on foot back along the road, through a trail
of plastic shopping bags, spilled cash, now-pointless food, the
purpose of the man's errand strewn and scattered, paltry there
for all to see.

We come to where he came to rest; I see his blood-red lips
and chalky face, and in his eyes a point-blank look, awake, agape.
A startled flock of terrors soars within me: he's still alive. His
chest heaves beneath the thin white T-shirt, his every fought-for
breath insisting: *not-dead, not-dead, not-dead.* A happenstance nurse
has already commandeered the scene, and she kneels beside him.

She asks his name; I don't hear his answer, but then she repeats it: *Dennis*. Others crouch there, and I can see there isn't room for me. I wish that I could do, or go. I don't want to simply stand there.

Panic ricochets from his eyes to mine and back again, and as the police arrive and the paramedics with their bags begin to run, I remember something one could do. I gather up my voice and call to the nurse who kneels at his side: "Hold his hand." And so she does. His fingers curl around hers before the swarm is on him.


2.   Virginia

A few weeks later my boyfriend and I are driving on the same stretch of road, and—what are the chances?—we see a car oddly parked on the median strip. A man is trying to push it to the side of the road. My boyfriend says, "I should at least go help that guy. You stay here."

Our own hazard lights blink and click as I watch, poised, until I hear my boyfriend call my name, and then I climb out and run in my pretty heels. A woman is in the driver's seat, her hands gripping the steering wheel. The two men are questioning her: where does she hurt, what happened? Remembering Dennis and the nurse just a few weeks ago, I lean in the window toward her and say gently, "What's your name?" "Virginia," she gasps. I say her name aloud and tell her, "Help will be here very soon" (and other empty words whose only value is their warm calm tone). I take her hand. She clutches mine with both her own, as if I were a long-lost friend showing up on her doorstep, bringing news she is profoundly relieved to hear.

When the paramedics arrive, they pull at me as if it is I who doesn't know that it's OK to let go. At this moment they don't know that the power is coming from her. I'm a total stranger but I've said her name and held her hand, and although they're the ones who will manage the situation, it's her grasp of me that they must work to pry away.

\* \* \*

*The Useless Thing*

In the car, I turn my face to the pane
Without sound and know
This useless thing
Is everything.
Because I was simply there
With Dennis and Virginia,
I could give those two
The thing I could not give to you.

Why did no one come along
To brave your face
Or ask your name
Or even touch your fingertip,
To see you off?

Why did no one stop their car
And run to you, and let you know
They would at least have this to give:
They'd stay with you and hold
   your hand,
Although you would not live?

# Lingering Thoughts on Discovery

W e're really on our own now, realizing the details of what happened to our lost person and the details of what's happening to our own life.

There are times of isolation: others can't accompany us on the most personal part of grief and mourning, because we're each the only one in our particular relationship with the deceased.

On a forced march to a place we don't want to go, we're getting very tired now. Endurance comes from nowhere. It begins when we stop waiting for deliverance from pain and just try something, take a step in a direction, any direction, maybe with no faith in anything more than the idea that we don't know what's next.

We begin to comprehend more fully the magnitude of what we've lost. We get our first sense of what it means that the loss is truly permanent—our loved one is *still* not coming back. And we discover that the one thing there's no exhaustion for is missing them.

# Treasure

## CHAPTER 28

# Words That Start With "Re-"

### (The Permanence of Change)

fter many months, I remove *A Secret History* from my kitchen table and place it, still open to page 326, into a box. I will never read another word of it. This could be just a willful refusal to continue reading a book I'm perfectly capable of reading. It could be a way of making sure that life *doesn't* merely continue exactly as before: if I had to lose him, then I'll make sure other things will change too, just on principle.

Or maybe I'm literally incapable of finishing the book—maybe I would tear like a mishandled page if I even tried. It's not that I don't want to find out what happens in the novel; my natural curiosity will always want to find out. The problem is, I've become someone who does not *get to* find out. The outcome of the story, and the outcome of my life if that morning had passed uneventfully, belong together, and each will remain unknown to me. The unread words of *A Secret History* are part of a secret future, the one that would have been, but that now will go unlived.

I've read several encouraging treatises about recovery. These articles promise that although there are many things I feel I'll never be able to do again, one day I "will discover that, in fact, I can." (Sometimes this turns out to be true. Other times, it doesn't.) *People are designed to recover,* I read. And certainly my friends and colleagues are tentatively hopeful, after many months have passed. "How are you and your family?" a friend asks. "Have you regained a sense of peace? Have you started returning to your own life?" (*My own life?* I think. *Whose life have I been living? At least that's something we all agree on: this life I've been living definitely hasn't felt like my own. So then whose is it, and can I please have mine back?*)

Inevitably: "You can't bring him back. You have to pick up where you left off." (I wish I could explain: *The first part of that is true, but there's no such thing as picking up where you left off. You can't bring a lost person back, but neither can you go back to your own old life, even though you'd hock your soul to do it. Why can't you go back? Because that version of you doesn't exist anymore.*)

And always, someone offers what they probably believe to be a gentle-but-wise reminder: "He's gone." (*Yes. So am I.*)

*  *  *

We've been confused, trying to live a life with the lost person still alive in it. We know the life we had is already wrecked and finished but we've been unable to conceive of any other way. We keep trying, long after we stop talking about it. (When someone seriously injured finally passes out from the pain, is it safe to assume he must be all well, because the cries of agony have ceased?) We keep trying to live that old life, even as we try to adjust to the new one. People judge our efforts at this, but we need privacy from that judgment. Words like *recover*, *return*, and *regain* suggest a restoration of chaos into its previous order, and to think we can do this is to nurture a delusion. If we're going to live sanely in the present day, it helps to acknowledge this: sometimes there can be no "re-."

*Advice to Advisors*

Don't wait for me,
Don't watch for me to reappear.
Don't be patient
Don't be steadfast
Don't linger in hope where I was
    last seen.
Don't believe that I will rejoin you,
To go on as we were before.

It's hard to accept,
But your pleas are no use.
The self that I was—
The me that you knew?
I know it's hard and
I know you don't want to,
But you must
Come to terms and
Let *that* me go.

# CHAPTER 29

# Walking the Tracks

(Paradox: The Sameness and the Uniqueness of Grief)

When my brothers and I were growing up, we loved to climb up the railroad bank across the street from our dad's parents' house in Wilkes-Barre, Pennsylvania. From this vantage point, we could see the Susquehanna River. A bit nearer lay a vast spread of coal-black debris we christened the Sea of Embers (which eventually gave up its poetic blackness to the construction of new housing developments), and of course directly underfoot were the tracks themselves. The dark wooden ties stretched into the distance with dizzying monotony, held together by two slender rails, each one rusted along the sides but nickel-shiny in the center from the rush and press of freight-train wheels. The soothing sameness of those tracks was a novelty we never quite got enough of.

Walking the tracks, when done in company, is the truest kind of parallel interaction, completely unlike sitting around a table facing each other. There are no crowds and no clamor, and not much in the way of social regulations. You don't have to look at anything in particular, or be looked at. You needn't keep up your end of the conversation; you can be there as a full participant even if you don't feel like saying a word, and no one so much as remarks upon your quiet. You can point out interesting flora and fauna, or toss in a question like a pebble into a pond, and listen to the way the conversational ripples widen. And there might be plain silence except for the sound of everyone traipsing. It's pressureless freedom. Ease.

Ease, but not necessarily mindlessness. When you climb up there, you discover that the scenery that looks so uniform from down on the roads is constantly shifting: these trees for those weeds, these roots for those rocks, here a view of houses, now a road, a glimpsed shimmer of river, sometimes the sound of a Martz bus on its way to the nearby terminal, and if you're lucky, the momentary dark orchestra of a train: clanging metal sidings and creaking wheels, followed by quiet—which in summertime is instantly overrun by the cacophony of cicadas and katydids, their vigorous calls serrating the air.

And it's not necessarily easy, either. The process of walking the tracks, the rhythm of taking steps, gets interesting the moment you realize you can't actually establish any rhythm at all. Each wooden tie is unique in size and shape and position, by turns dried and warped in the sun, or damp and mildewy in cold grey weather, smoothed by rain or gouged to erratic splinters the size of hunting knives, half-buried in the stones or sitting almost on top of them, and spaced either too far apart or not far apart enough to fit your stride. Among the rocks between the ties is an astonishing medley of debris, from broken glass to bottle caps, pebbles of purplish taconite ore and river-polished stones, fast food rubbish, skeletons of unidentifiable small animals, soda can pull-tabs, starling feathers, lost mittens, ancient shards of dog-gnawed tennis balls, stray lost bits of every type and sort—things upon which you wouldn't necessarily want to tread. Every single footfall is managed and felt. You can get good at it, but still, you don't get bored up here the way you can when you're walking on a smooth, predictable road. Always, some part of you must attend to the simple act of stepping.

Maybe this is why walking the tracks absorbs restlessness: it combines the fascination of novelty with the calm of sameness. Underneath all the temporary upsets, the comings and goings of trains, storms, bugs, trash, weeds, and seasons, something imperturbable abides. Agitation can be waited out; the railroad and its banks are characterized by ever-renewing unchangingness. It's the same always but never stagnant. No matter how much time goes by, the railroad bank is weeds and wooden ties and passing boxcars, but each weed and wooden tie and passing boxcar is unique; each step is shaped differently from the one before. In a given moment, whether you perceive uniqueness or sameness, steadiness or change, merely depends on how you look at it.

* * *

When someone young dies, there's a sameness, a predictability to our reactions. "Only the good die young," someone always says. Obituaries describe lovable personalities with shining talents—she was "so bright and friendly to everyone," or he was "so talented, so athletic," as if these were somehow exceptional. No one ever says, "Gosh, a great kid but basically indistinguishable from a million others who are good at math or baseball or graphic arts or all three," or "Very friendly but with tastes similar to those of every teenager in the tri-state area..." When we're not the ones grieving, we notice the sameness of grief. Then why do we suffer so acutely the loss of an individual who, on paper or from the slightest distance, would appear to others to be like countless other people? Why is one person special to us and anonymous to others, among so many individuals who are precious to others but anonymous to us?

In Antoine de Ste. Exupéry's *The Little Prince*, the little prince asks the fox a question about this. The prince is wondering why he loves his particular rose plant when there are thousands of other roses in the universe. The fox tells him that what makes his specific flower matter so much is the "time that you have wasted" for it. In *The Art of Loving*, Erich Fromm writes something similar, explaining that "one loves that for which one labors, and one labors for that which one loves." We live as individuals, with our intensely personal concerns and affections. Whomever we've specifically related to, put the time in to get to know, becomes special to us.

But in doing this, we're just like all other people, who likewise have personal concerns and affections. For all our superficial differences, people are remarkably alike in the ways we learn to love others, and in how we respond to momentous things in life, including loss.

At times in grief, we transcend our uniqueness, and consequently our isolation, by looking at how similar we are to others who have lost a person dear to them. At other times, we transcend the sense of sameness and replaceability by zeroing in on specifics, the traits and stories that make our own lost person a limited edition of *one*. (God may be in the details—but so is each one of us.) In a given moment, whether we're unique or universal merely depends on how we look at things.

## Chapter 30

# Artist-in-Resonance

(Fear of Remembering)

*The double grief of a lost bliss*
*Is to recall its happy hour in pain.*
—Dante Alighieri, *The Inferno*

I've long since gone back to my usual routine, but it has lost a certain coherence. The specifics of life now feel like a disassembled song, as if without that one particular note, all the rest have fallen apart and are sounding randomly. The old melodies won't play. What's supposed to happen now?

One is, I understand, supposed to "deal with it" and "come to terms"—casual, slangy phrases that hang around as if they're self-explanatory but that are rarely explained. "Integrate the loss," a textbook will say; "incorporate it into ongoing life." But again, what are the instructions? *How* exactly does one do this, on a practical, day-to-day, minute-to-minute basis? With willingness to be attentive to the present day some of the time, and lost in memory other times. With willingness to do things in spite of the loss, and to do things because of it. To alternate; to intersperse. It's as good an approach as any.

The things I do "in spite of" the loss: shopping, cleaning, paying the bills, working at the office, doing the laundry, taking a dance lesson, reading books, going out to dinner, seeing movies, making an appointment to get taxes done, spending half an hour on hold in order to straighten out a medical insurance mess, asking a coworker where she got her excellent shoes, listening to a friend tell about how his daughter will be on TV. As far as doing things "because of" the loss—I pick things that seem worthwhile and that remind me of my brother, things he might have liked: He frequented thrift stores and he had a soft spot for homeless people, so I donate to the Salvation Army. I take little trips with family members to scout out his graffiti, take pictures, admire the colors, the technique, and the brilliant nerve of it. This is my best effort at simple interspersing.

It turns out not to be so simple at all, though, because of how easy it is to be overwhelmed by the slightest thing that puts me in mind of him. I look at some random object, or overhear a bit of meaningless conversation in line at the supermarket, and I'm paralyzed without warning. The most trivial, almost irrelevant thing can set off symphonies of reminiscence. I see a piano in a store window and in an instant, I see myself as a young adult at the family piano and my youngest-but-tallest brother sitting on the couch behind me with his banjo, an unplanned duet of *She'll Be Comin' Round the Mountain* in progress but with at least ten tries for both of us to get it right and both of us laughing saying "Oops — no — wait!" and *both of us stagefright and wow he taught himself to play that thing-he's a college student-letters-paintings-(he kept that silly picture of a white lab-rat saying "hi" that I drew on scrap paper with blue highlighter)-he had so many MagicMarkers-skateboard-hisgreencar-incomprehensible-talent (when did he start smoking) and his sense of humor like goosefeathers but now he's gone and whywhywhy and all the unfairly lost marvel of this one person.* All that from the sight of a random piano.

The effect is overpowering, for a long time. I'm supposed to "integrate the loss" with this going on? It's like trying to walk down the street with every note of birdsong touching off a crescendo of cathedral bells. The symbols and reverberations are out of control. The volume is too high, the sounds too gut-twisting; there's too much feedback; nothing to do but stand still, and wince, and wait.

* * *

The word *resonance* comes from the Latin *resonare*, "to resound." It has specific meanings in chemistry and physics, but in everyday life we think of it in terms of music. The wires of a piano will resonate when one of their own key is played. If the middle C is played, the upper C– and lower C–pitched strings will move too, although they haven't been touched directly. They're said to vibrate "in sympathy." It's a good metaphor for the way songs, words, and images reach across time and space, carrying meanings that stir up recognition even if we've never seen those images or heard those songs before: *I know that feeling. That melody is exactly what I would compose if I knew how. That poem says it perfectly. I love that picture.* We say we're moved, or "touched," by something—as if we ourselves were resonating.

With each passing day, we become increasingly sensitized to the slightest reminder of our lost person, as though fewer and fewer brushstrokes can suggest an entire portrait to our sensitized eyes, the way a few opening notes can suggest an entire song. Now, when a single memory-string is plucked, the music always seems to end up in a minor key, as though every memory is a weapon turned against us. We can look at photos all we want, review all our symbols and mementos, try to connect with our lost person and feel comforted, but to no avail—we feel overwhelming pain. We're pining.

For a long time, our loved one's death overwhelms any other thoughts we have of them, and this mixing of two ideas—the person and their death—may drive us to avoid both altogether. We're afraid we won't be able to withstand the pain of having lost them. We're afraid we'll never be able to think of them without being paralyzed by the fact of their death. Should we stop actively remembering all the details of this person, to blunt our awareness of how painful life is without them? Pining is ever-renewing pain—think of our memories, think about the loss, agonize; repeat. It seems futile.

But there might be a purpose to pining. Do we listen to a song only once and never again, because we "already heard that one"? Do we read a poem or a story only once and then vow never to reread it because it affected us too much? People build entire careers on interpretation and reinterpretation of art or literature or music, perennial replayings of the same concertos and arias, rereading of books and writing new commentaries on ancient paintings, restudying works by artists long since dead who will never produce anything new. We buy music and play it repeatedly. We don't ignore a beautiful picture once we've seen it for the first time—we hang it up and look at the same image, day after day, and take delight in it. We love something all the more, the more we return to it...sometimes because it's a known pleasure, but sometimes because we're comforted or inspired by it, and sometimes because it seems to speak of something we recognize but can't articulate for ourselves. Our favorite things speak to us differently according to our frame of mind when we're taking them in. We don't cast them out because of the intensity—we go back to them again and again *because* they make us feel something, because they resonate with us so strongly.

Maybe pining isn't useless...maybe what we're doing is a "re-" that's still possible: revisiting. It's intensely painful, but we also know on some level that if a single line of melody is a tripwire for anguished nostalgia, at other times, it might strike equally powerful chords of delight. It takes time to become skilled in the strange art of resonance, skilled in perceiving a lifetime and scaling wall after wall of emotion within a few seconds of a momentary reminder. It takes a long time to learn to endure—let alone appreciate—the reverberating cathedral bells that a single note of birdsong touches off. Like a student of any art, we start off overwhelmed.

## CHAPTER 31

# As the Sunflower

(Fear of Forgetting)

*The heart that has truly loved never forgets,*
*But as truly loves on to the close,*
*As the sunflower turns on her god as he sets*
*The same look which she turned when he rose.*
　　—Thomas Moore, "Believe Me, If All Those
　　　Endearing Young Charms"

One evening, as I'm having dinner with a boyfriend at a restaurant called Old Country Buffet, a young man walks in who's tall and slim, with glasses and curly brown hair. This is perfectly unremarkable, but he also has a certain lope to his stride, and there is an indefinable wistfulness in the way he holds his shoulders. And there's a look of held-back humor in his face as he talks to his companions. I don't say anything to my own companion, but I'm transfixed; I glance at the young man's face several times, trying to be discreet but fascinated nonetheless by his resemblance to my lost brother.

I resist the temptation to accidentally meet this stranger at the ice cream machine, because he's himself, not my brother. If this guy is like most people, he probably wouldn't want to be singled out solely because he looks like another person. Who wants to be greeted this way: "Hi, I'm being friendly only because you look like someone else and in fact I wish you were that other person instead of who you are"…? It's the ultimate in looking through someone, seeing not their unique self but only their resemblance to someone else.

At the same time, I'm glad this guy is here even if I don't meet him, because unknowingly, he's reminded me of something. Not for a second have I forgotten that my brother had similar features, a similar walk, a similar silhouette. But what I have forgotten is the beautiful take-it-for-granted casualness of seeing those things in a living, moving, speaking person who's right here in the same room with me.

My mind suddenly flies to my stash of sympathy cards, to a theme that pops up over and over and is clearly meant to be a reassurance: as long as someone is remembered, the cards say soothingly, then the person is "never truly dead." But there is something ominous about this sentiment. It suggests that as long as we remember him, he's somehow safe, somehow not as dead as he would be if we suppressed our memories or just went on our way. As if forgetting were an offense people could commit against him, a form of neglect. And this leads to a disturbing idea: What if I get completely distracted about something? What if I'm watching a show about the rarified lives of aspiring ballerinas in Paris, or studying a website about hip action in samba, or just enjoying being immersed in some other topic my friends and family wouldn't be the faintest bit interested in, and I don't think about my little brother at all? And here's something no greeting card would even attempt to address: Of all the people who cared about him, what if I'm the last one left alive, the only one around to remember, and then I get dementia or a head injury and forget vast quantities of my life and his? Does that mean I will have "truly" killed him? Does my own distraction or forgetfulness consign him to an existential trash dump?

No, it doesn't. This is why the deeper pain of loss is not eased by those greeting cards. My little brother isn't resurrected or kept alive—as sweet as that idea is—if only I remember him faithfully enough. But neither is he "more" dead, his existence obliterated, if I forget. His death can never erase the fact that he lived. His existence is already true, beyond the power of anything the rest of us do or forget to do. As in so many other aspects of his death, we're all powerless, but in this case it's a comfort.

In the restaurant, for politeness's sake, I stop trying to steal glances at the guy who looks like my brother. My date is talking to me, and so I bring my attention back to the here and now. Unconsciously my hand goes to my neck, to the tiny heart-shaped locket I wear that has a miniature picture of my little brother hidden inside it. The locket gently buzzes as I scroll it back and forth on its chain, in what has already become a habit as natural as twirling my hair.

\* \* \*

At war with the pain of remembering is the fear of forgetting. At first, we're unable to control where our thoughts go, no matter how much we try to exert our will over them. We know in general, though, that without reminders or practice or review, the brain is likely to let details slip out of awareness. In grief, we might let this happen on purpose because it allows us refuge from pain that would otherwise be intolerable. Yet we don't want to feel bad at the sight of any reminder of the person themselves. On the contrary, we want the thought of them to make us feel good, not bad. Are we doomed to feel good only if we "forget" reality?

We have a complicated relationship with the idea of forgetting, and what it means. To forget is to lose our awareness of the past. Is it an act we commit? Or a passive thing that happens to us, with or without our consent? Over many months, it gets easier to guide our thoughts—there might be less of a need to squash them, and instead we start shepherding them as if they are stray animals with a tendency to wander unchecked. We can preserve a mental space where we put our attention squarely on the person, absence and all, so that at other times we can attend to other things, without guilt or panic.

This seems like a healthy thing, but we might secretly be uneasy about our increasing skill at it. Maybe we sense some dreadful meaning, as if by learning to postpone the expression of sadness, it means we're "cheering up" and have somehow begun to care less. Are we betraying the deceased? It's easy to get confused about what it means to forget, versus what it means to distract, or to set certain thoughts aside on purpose for a while.

Directing our attention elsewhere, on purpose or by accident, doesn't mean we've forgotten. It means our minds deal with thoughts on a rotating basis. Often, we need to set grief aside for a while because we're responsible for something in the present moment—taking a final exam, driving on a freeway in rush hour, comforting a sick child, fixing a broken china teapot, or operating on someone's eye.

When we're kids, trial-and-error teaches us when to reveal our thoughts, when to save their expression for later, and whom (if anyone) to share them with. Now, again, we learn to choose the direction of our thoughts of the lost person, when to express those thoughts, and when to keep them to ourselves. This balancing act takes practice, but it doesn't mean we forget. Even if we *do* forget, no matter what the reason, our lost person is not affected. The reality of them will never depend on other people's attention, or even on our own frail memories.

But still. It's not in our power to keep someone alive who has died, but we want to "keep them alive" in our mental world. To let all the details escape our memories would feel too much like losing them again...and there are things we can do to prevent that. It might be as simple as noticing how a stranger resembles the person we miss. We visit gravesites and memorials, and we keep things that we can look at, hold in our hands, or wear on a little chain around our neck. We save things that belonged to that person, and we cherish something as authentic and unique as a snippet of their hair, a photograph of their face, a picture they drew, or something they wrote. Such things are proof that they were here, saw that, went there, did this, created that, thought this way or that way about the world. Keepsakes give us pangs, momentary respites, laughs, and send us into stratospheres of reverie, and we love the idea that they'll still be here even after we ourselves are long gone. They now represent our lost person's presence in the physical world, and so we carry them around as tokens of a loyalty that is very much alive.

The safeguarding of memory is the beginning of our apprenticeship in the art of resonance. With a keepsake, or any reminder that we deliberately keep among our possessions, we continue a relationship with our own memories. We can choose to place our thoughts on a simple little object, and contemplate everything (*so-much-everything...*) it calls to mind.

## Chapter 32

# Something New

(Fear of Losing the Future)

*You have always been in others and you will remain in others. And what does it matter to you if later on that is called your memory? This will be you—the you that enters the future and becomes a part of it.*

—Boris Pasternak, *Dr. Zhivago*

When my mother was expecting Matt, we older kids asked if she was planning to wear one of those witty T-shirts for pregnant women that read "Under Construction," with an arrow pointing to the pregnancy bump. "That's a little too obvious for me," she said. So instead she wore one that read, simply, "Something New."

Something new—this is the crux, now. It's what we're most exquisitely aware that we'll never have again, with Dave. When I contemplate the loss of the Dave-containing future, my keepsake objects don't always help. Those objects are all from the past; I'm too aware that there will never be any *new* objects, new interactions, new jokes or difficulties, frustrations, happy events, or funny stories—things that should have happened but won't.

One night I dream I'm having a conversation with my brother. It's a conversation that never occurred while he was alive, but it's not what he says that makes it so memorable. It's that like any dream, it seems so *real*. It's worth the pain of awakening, because just for those moments, I was living in that parallel universe in which the car didn't swerve and he's still alive. I was in the future that had him in it.

I go walking on train tracks along a passenger line called SEPTA, which connects Philadelphia to its suburbs. With me is Warren, a friend of Matt and Dave's. He's taking me to see a sample of my brother's graffiti, not a hasty scribble but a fully realized image known in street-art parlance as a "piece" (short for "masterpiece"). Warren speaks ceaselessly as we walk the tracks, and we both look over our shoulders every minute or so, because this is a weekday on an active commuter line, and speeding trains can approach from either direction at any time.

When at last we come to our destination, we stand and look at Dave's graffiti piece. It looks like he'd opened a kaleidoscope, made a spinning mobile out of its contents (sky blue and pale peach letters ablaze at their edges with vivid marine and deep orange), then pressed the whole thing against a wall in a fever-dream of madly intentional creation. Slightly grotesque like much of his art, it's ordered enough to show some of the letters—ARS—in his graffiti tag, but chaotic enough to be disturbing and nearly alive. It confuses the eye; only M.C. Escher could follow it; it's a tangle of colors about to move on its own in some weird frolic the very moment you turn your back. This spray-paint-on-concrete image definitely belongs in no museum but right here where it is, among the rocks and the miles of track and the trains flying through and the suspenseful quiet in between, and the high-voltage wires strung overhead and the signs warning of danger. The piece practically hums.

Of course Warren and I don't say these things; we just mill around and casually scuff our feet against the stones, and gaze at the painted wall. After we've given it its full meed of admiration, we simply turn around and trek all the way back along the tracks until we emerge into the parking lot of the Fort Washington train station. We cross the street to Friendly's Restaurant. At the takeout window, I order a dish of mint chocolate chip ice cream, and Warren sits on the curbstone next to me while I eat it. He has maintained what has been essentially a monologue without interruption since we set out. I eat ice cream; he talks.

Alternately hilarious and unnerving, Warren's stories are about their shenanigans as friends. In the space of a few hours, Warren fills in aspects of Dave's life that I'd never been privy to, because I'd been away at college, at work, back at school, back at work, moving through the elliptical orbits of my own life. Some of the things Warren tells me I suspect I probably shouldn't know, but I'm honored that he trusts me to take things in stride as a keeper of certain sibling-level knowledge. I let some of the details dissipate from my memory immediately and file the rest away under a mental category of Evidence That Dave Wasn't a Cherub. I'm glad there's more to my brother than I'll ever know; that's the way it should be.

I don't see Warren again after that day, but it's reassuring to know that he and Dave's other friends (and family members and teachers and classmates and managers and served customers, for that matter) are out there in the world somewhere, full of stories I'll never hear.

* * *

A future has been lost. How does a person mourn experiences that never happened; how can we mourn the loss of something we never had in the first place? How do we grieve something as elusive and indefinable as thwarted expectations? How can we reconcile ourselves to never having anything new?

The experiences we'd looked forward to may not have happened, but the anticipation itself has already happened; it happens every time we envision something. Just as powerful as our intangible hopes are our actual dreams. Mental images that appear in a dream feel real because we haven't consciously designed them, and we can't usually control them. Within our own unreachable minds, people who have died in the physical world may continue to exist and interact with us.

We may chide ourselves about "believing" our dreams, or being consoled by them: It was just a figment of our over-wrought imagination. A trick, something cheap and under-handed, perpetrated upon itself by a mind that is at once both crafty and credulous. But what is a dream, or an imagination? Psychologists tell us that when we're facing a challenge, we can affect the outcome by envisioning ourselves succeeding. An athlete is encouraged to visualize strong performance; a speech will go better if we practice it in our minds; a person with cancer may be stunned to find his health improving when he practices imagining healthy cells destroying the cancer cells. The mind can guide the body and change the way it experiences the outside world. If thoughts can soothe or stoke our anxiety, heal or exacerbate our illness, and affect our performance, it's no surprise that our thoughts and dreams can also assuage grief...if we accept the comfort instead of scorning it. It doesn't matter if the athlete's vision isn't "real"—the effect on the body, the improved performance, is real. It doesn't matter if the cancer sufferer's imaginings are fantasies; the effect on the body, healing from illness, is unmistakable. It doesn't matter if the content of a dream is not happening in waking life. The *effect* of it—a moment of comfort—is true.

Outside our own heads is another trove of newness: other people who knew our loved person and had a relationship with them entirely separate from our own, memories entirely different from our own, and expectations of a future with the lost person in it. When we listen to these people talk about our lost person, we learn new things and may find ourselves crowing in delight or clucking in dismay. We're wandering in that mirror-hall of memory again, only this time, we're wandering in company and we have new encounters with memories that don't belong specifically to us. We're glad for the new light these other people shed on someone we've both lost but will not give up. Our mutual loss has introduced us and, like a skilled host, can recede from present-day conversation without either of us forgetting why we met, that first thing we ever had in common. We take our leave of each other, knowing that all different kinds of lamps of memory for the lost person are lit and carried—here, there, and everywhere.

## CHAPTER 33

# Unwanted Belongings

(The Fellowship of Loss)

I receive a card from an ex-colleague named Sue who lost her own brother years ago. It's a short note. There's a lot I don't need to say to her, or she to me.

A longtime family friend, Marge, visits my parents frequently. Our two families have known each other for many years, and when she heard about my brother, she herself was still reeling from the recent and sudden loss of her husband, Chuck. With the gentle instinct of someone who is herself still in fresh mourning, she sends me cards with handwritten notes, sometimes with a carefully copied poem or quote that she hopes will offer consolation. Her looping handwriting is a slightly random combination of printing and cursive script (like mine, but neater), and the sight of it is as comforting as the words she writes. Maybe even more so.

\* \* \*

There's this group of others with whom we have an instant kinship: people grieving a loss similar to ours. We don't want to belong to this category but we have no choice; we belong whether we like it or not. Encountering these others who have lost someone dear to them is a way to practice living with the truth, alongside other people having just as hard a time with a similar truth. We understand each other's pain with a disturbing accuracy: no forced positivity ("It's OK...") because it's *not* OK. No false optimism ("Everything will be all right") because in fact everything will *not* be all right. It's a relief to be around people who understand that sometimes platitudes can be stifling. These people know that vague reassurances may be polite, but they aren't true. It takes guts to know this: things will never quite be "all right" again.

When we're in this little community, our presence, rather than being a grim reminder, is instead a comfort to the other reluctant members. We don't want this skill, or grace, or whatever it is—but we have it, and so do they. It's a community based, ironically, on something that all of us *don't have*. It's a fellowship based on absences.

The details always differ, of course. If we talk to ten people who've each lost someone, we rediscover that our situation is unique and we're alone in it. No one thing is a comfort to everyone. Our own "quiet, peaceful image" will be the match to a powder keg for someone else. Sitting by a lake where you used to go fishing with your lost loved one may soothe your grief, but for someone else whose beloved drowned in that lake, the symbolism is very different. And if it's your own loved one who drowned in the lake where you'd previously spent many happy hours fishing together, then the meaning of that lake is different yet again.

But beyond the specifics, we get each other on a level that strangers normally wouldn't even attempt. It's the opposite of being artificially set apart; we're inadvertently, suddenly, kindred. This bond defies the usual rules about closeness requiring time to develop. After five minutes of conversation with someone who has had a loss of similar magnitude, we can comprehend a thousand things about each other in the most immediate and vivid way. It comes from knowing what it's like to have a missingness as a central element in life.

In this group, we encounter sympathetic listeners who listen to us as we describe the details. Misery doesn't "love" company; what misery needs is support. When we tell our story, for a moment we're eased of our burden. By telling our story, by being the bearer of the news, we temporarily displace our role of hapless unwary victim onto someone else, who then takes the blow. It's a fraction of a second of not-me-this-time.

We tell our story a thousand times because we need to say the words, and then one day, we change roles and find ourselves sharing for the sake of someone else, to help them feel understood. Then we stop talking and listen to their story, and we take the blow for them so that they get a momentary relief, a fraction of a second of not-me-this-time. We carry a bit of each other's pain away, trading and sharing, and this becomes a way out of hopeless suffering. Sharing grief doesn't stop us going out of our mind. It stops us getting too far into it.

## Chapter 34

# Mental Cigarettes

(Pause)

D ave was a smoker; my mother has given me one of his empty Marlboro packs. I put it into a little basket along with a picture of him, one of his paintbrushes, and a few other things I look at every day. I've often wondered how smokers manage to give up the habit, not for the cigarettes alone, but also for the cigarette break—the tiny ritual in every cigarette that creates its own space, a little way station on the road of daily life. The smoke swirling upward silently has always seemed to represent the smoker's thoughts dissolving into the air, unreadable by anyone else, impossible to recapture in their original form. Even watching someone else have a cigarette break is a kind of pause that gives a bit of quiet, a moment apart from the clamor of time, or from the chatter and squawk of a restless mind. I always wondered if the end of the cigarette break, the eventual emergence from within that tiny cloud, brought not just a nicotine hit but a new clarity about anything.

I used to wonder if smoking would have made it easier to get through medical school. The students who were smokers would gather outside in the courtyard with random doctors, nurses, and wheelchair-bound patients with IVs in their arms, hanging out in motley groups. I didn't particularly want to smoke, but I liked the idea of a permissible respite, and it seemed alluring to take just a couple drags before plunging back into the fray of being a medical student, a nurse, a doctor, or a patient, all of whom are strung out by the intensity of life in a hospital.

My outpatient pediatrics rotation was one of the lower-intensity months, involving mostly sore throats and ear infections. One day stands out vividly, though, one of the few days I would gladly have been a smoker, if only to regain my calm after a singular morning. Before we started the day's schedule of office hours, I followed the attending physician on rounds at the hospital across the street. He didn't have many in-patients; in the early hours we discussed the day's only new admission, a six-month-old boy named Michael. This patient was hospitalized because he'd been physically abused, and the police were coming to photograph his injuries for legal purposes. Steeling ourselves for a difficult morning, the pediatrician and I went to Michael's room.

There in a crib lay an infant with marble-pale skin and the faintest dandelion-fuzz of blond hair. But instead of the usual fussiness or gurgling and cooing characteristic of a six-month-old, this baby had already learned not to make a sound, regardless of what was done to him. The nurses said it was "strange" how he never cried. Instead he took in the world through eyes the size of newborn planets. Many people have eyes that can speak; his were listening. Hearkening. In the compass of that huge gaze, I reached into the crib and lifted him out as carefully as if I were ten years old again, standing before a bassinette. I thought of a poem by George MacDonald: *Where did you come from, baby dear? Out of the everywhere, into the here.*

Michael was harrowingly compliant as the ancient Polaroid camera whirred and popped in blue-white flashes. My invisible heart had already broken open and was oozing like an egg dropped on stone, but in order to protect him from my own distress, I murmured to him in as calm a voice as I could manage.

"Little pumpkin, baby-sweet..." The officers needed pictures from different angles, so I shifted him slowly in case any of those mute bruises still hurt. When the photographs were finished, I smoothed Michael's downy head and nuzzled it with a helpless gesture, trying to give him some sort of comfort as I handed him back to the nurses. The broken egg was a runny mess by then, but I was already trained to hide within myself, with no giveaways in the professional façade except quietude in the midst of the ceaseless clinical hubbub, and a memory of love-in-passing for a brutalized baby boy I never saw again.

The memory of him stayed. It's a humble kind of grief, to pity a child who is living but who has been uncherished, mistreated, abused. Thinking of this now, I understand that the innocent six-month-old Michael had lost the very first baby lottery. I'm hopeful that Matt and Dave would judge that they hadn't.

* * *

In grief, there are many pauses, some forced upon us and some that we've deliberately sought out. It might be a cigarette break, a coffee break, a two-month break, or a mental break from the here and now. The pauses aren't blank, though. They're full of time to recognize, to consider more slowly, to look more lingeringly at what has passed before us. They're full of time to become more aware, and to see more clearly.

## CHAPTER 35

# The Envy of the Angels

(Irrevocable Things To Be Glad Of)

I want to make something to commemorate my little brother, although as of yet I have no idea what. I've managed the poem for the funeral, and I know that one day I'll write again for his memory, but for now I'm not ready for words.

Music? Tim and Mike have each made compilations of songs for the rest of us, and I play my copies every few days, for weeks at a time. But for me, music is incapacitating—trying to create a montage with it is like trying to sip from a geyser; I'm quickly deluged.

Dave was alive the last time I made something for him. It hangs on my wall now: a pencil drawing I'd started several years ago, of him as a little kid. I'd wanted to give him a present although I hadn't any clear thought of what the present would be for. I'd just wanted to draw a picture of him, for him.

There were two photos I'd considered using, both of him at about age one. In the first, he's in his Sunday best, a white sweater with a red and black stripe. He's half turned away, looking back into the camera. The photo is slightly overexposed, the pale skin seraphic, eyes warm brown, brows so light they're like whispers, brown curls brushed into semi-tidiness. He's wearing the gentlest of smiles, unexpected in someone so young, as if he were kindly indulging the photographer's wish to capture his image.

The photo makes me sad, the unearthly glow and the momentariness of it—the smile is clear-eyed but it's a look back; he's headed somewhere else, one shoulder already in shadow.

He's the same age in the other photo, but otherwise it's entirely different. This one shows an earthy, irresistible, giggly toddler clad in a red T-shirt and denim jacket. Straight into the camera comes his uninhibited laugh, four baby-teeth visible on top, only two on the bottom, so small they're like little toy teeth. Silky brown curlicues are rioting across his high white forehead, and his gaze is fully engaged with the camera in an instant of perfect joy. I imagined that for him, as for many people, this unguarded happiness was rare, so I chose that photo.

I worked on the portrait for weeks, sitting in the most posturally reprehensible ways, sideways on the couch with my face inches from the drawing pad, my shoulder blades scrunched in a paroxysm of concentration. Then I started getting headaches from the hours of fierce focus. I let the project sit in the corner of my couch for several months. I moved to a different apartment. I worked on the portrait again through the early months of 2004, but the further along I got with it, the more apprehensive I became. It had to do with why I felt the need to give him this present. Mainly, it was motivated by a dark fear that I couldn't explain:

*I tell my friend Lisa about my anxiety for him, my inexplicable fear for his well-being. It's founded less on specifics, I tell her, but more on a general feeling. Unsure if I'm being ridiculous, completely misreading a situation, succumbing to some ghastly gear-slip of my own melancholy mind, I prevaricate, argue the pros and cons of doing this drawing-as-gift, unsure how to bestow it. Unsure if I even should. He and I have grown up and grown apart, evolving into very different lifestyles, and have become in some ways strangers who might want to get reacquainted, find out who we each were as adults. How would I explain my gift to him? He might think I was crazy, or maybe I'd create disquiet where there was none... but then he'd never know I was worried about him...maybe I'd simply alienate him? Lisa gently clamps a conversational fist down on the bleeding artery of my rambling, and goes carefully but unerringly to the point. "Judy," she says, her voice kind, her words measured, "listen to me: dead brother." She's aware that I understand her perfectly. We discuss what she means: no one knows for sure what will happen to anyone, so never mind all the fretting; if something bad ever did happen, how would you feel if you hadn't given him this gift? It's a hypothetical conversation and we both know I'm being absurd. She's only pointing out the fact that no one can predict the future, and a person can only act on present-moment inspiration. "You're right," I reply. "I can just give him something."*

So I kept going with it. In the spring of 2004, his approaching graduation from college seemed like the perfect opportunity to give him the gift-portrait. By early springtime I'd finished it, but his graduation wasn't until mid-May and I couldn't wait—I had to show it off to him, to hasten the moment when I'd dance the triumphant little jig reserved for those who have managed to orchestrate a perfect surprise. I drove over to my parents' house to present it to him still unframed, the paper not even torn from the drawing pad yet:

*He's not home at the moment, so I bring the tablet in to my parents' living room and prop it against the wall, and I wait for him. He gets home...I tell him I have something for him in the other room... for a moment our roles might be reversed, I'm so excited and hopeful of impressing him, like a little kid showing off a kindergarten art project...I lead him into the living room and unveil the portrait! He smiles, with the suggestion of a giggle (the way he would at other times, when I'd said something he thought was funny and he'd mumble through his own spluttering mirth, "Maff, did you hear what Judes just said?"). He's still smiling now. "Cool," he says, looking slightly bemused. Surprised, yeah, but not overly—I needn't have worried that he'd question me; we're from the same gene pool after all, which has always meant accepting even the most nonsensical creative effort as legitimate in its own right. I notice a flaw in the drawing as I set it on the dining room table, and then we're having a technical conversation about a tiny adjustment I'm trying to make to a shadow along the nose. This conversation is a threshold, the first conversation I have about art with my brother-the-artist. He asks if I'd found it difficult to work with pencils, given how they smudge so easily. I agree that I'd encountered that exact problem. We discuss how awkward it is, to stabilize the drawing hand without smearing anything—how tricky it is to poise the tip of your little finger against the paper, touching it but only just barely...but you have to find a way, carefully, if you want to keep adding to it without messing up what you've already got.*

He did not live the few weeks more to his own graduation. It's a story I don't tell aloud; its crown-jewel perfection is too fraught with a fragile, shimmering terror, the kind reserved for the very closest of close calls. The memory of that day, the sound and the smile of his unsurprised surprise when he first saw the picture, must be kept inviolate, because of what the memory means: if I'd waited to give him the portrait as a formal gift for his graduation, it would have been too late. The two phrases, "would have been" and "too late," each so ugly on its own, together are an accidental melody. An opportunity seized. One final chance, which I hadn't known would be final but which some instinct made me take.

Today there's the memory of the pencil portrait, alongside much earlier days of tiptoeing in to see newborn Matt, or of coming home from school to hear baby Dave, who called me Dee-dee back then, telling me to hide so he could seek. I was the envy of the angels at those times, and I knew it. I got to be Dave's sister. My parents got to be his parents; my other brothers got to be his brothers, his friends got to be his friends. He lived; we knew him. Every so often, that's all I know, and all I need to know.

* * *

For the newly bereaved, lost blessings are more lost than blessings. Sometimes it's salt in the wound, to be encouraged to "hold on to the good things, be grateful, count your blessings, cherish the memories." It's precisely all those cherishable things that have just disappeared. It's agonizing to hear that it's better to have loved and lost than never to have loved at all.

But even now, we can be surprisingly receptive to ideas that are irrevocable. The person was so perfectly him- or herself. In a way, he was ours. In a way, we were hers. These reflections, maybe because they're unassailable, bring a kind of quiet. They're truths that are safe from harm and won't change. If the things we regret can't be changed, the things we're glad of can't be changed either. These lighthouse-flashes of gratitude help us find our way as we head further into our damaged future.

## CHAPTER 36

# Spaced Between

### (An Alternative to Staying in the Moment or Spacing Out Altogether)

*The distinction between past, present, and future is only a stubbornly persistent illusion.*

—Albert Einstein

My books encourage the practice of being "in the moment." The past is fantasy. The future is invisible. The present moment, therefore, is extolled as the only legitimate place to be. But sometimes the thing we most hate to admit is what screams the loudest in our head: sometimes, the present moment is intolerable. Escapist activities, like watching three movies in a row or reading a novel instead of cleaning the bathroom, are temporary, and they're OK when my strength ebbs. I recognize the danger of potential addiction, how it's not a solution that will work out well. But sometimes I'm so fatigued by the relentlessness of grief that I need somewhere else to go, a state of mind that doesn't require me to pretend anything, a resting-point in reality that's not typically mentioned in the trinity of Past, Present, and Future. I stumble upon this place by accident, when I'm at my arts and crafts.

I've considered trying to paint something. It would be a fitting tribute to this brother of mine who could with equal ease paint an oil-on-canvas showing a trippy-colored, film-negative image of a girl, or a mural of grimacing vegetables lit up spookily from below (every single caricatured face unique, as in a crowd of actual people), or a subtly shaded graffiti-image of a disturbingly anthropomorphic grasshopper chewing on a carpet tack (in reference to a Leon Redbone song, brought into Dave's consciousness as a result of our dad's free-ranging musical tastes).

Just before the car crash, one of his classmates, Josh, made a short film of Dave demonstrating graffiti techniques. In the video, Josh's voice instructs my brother to explain how he approaches the creation of a piece; Dave's own unassuming and often mumbling voice then narrates. First, he says, find a good background and prepare it. (The camera shows the dingy backpack in which the cans of spray paint are secreted; he was in the habit of wrapping the cans in sweaters to muffle their clanking, a precaution that enabled him to skunk them past our parents or any other party who might interfere with these illegal artistic missions.) Dave's arm is shown spraying beige paint on a wall, to make a concrete canvas. He recommends a rough outline of the design you have in mind, in a light color "so it doesn't get too convoluted and you can't tell what you're doing." The next steps are to "fill it in...add whatever designs you want...sign and date it," and then add more of "whatever you want," he keeps saying. "Whatever you wanna do."

He makes it sound simple, but I have no experience with paint beyond watercolors as a kid, and the idea of working quickly in the night, keeping a wary eye out for police or for trains that might round a bend and squash me, gives me a palpitating anxiety. More to the point, I don't know the first thing about graffiti, and if I even thought about trying it, I'd be apprehended in a trice and slapped with a fine for Egregious Public Ridiculousness before I could say "poseur." Painting is his thing, not mine, and I'm not trying (or at least not consciously trying) to re-create or channel him; I'm trying to create something *for* him, *from* me.

However, although I'm not a painter, I am very interested in the *way* he painted. In this video, he works in a way that manages to be both furtive and confident at once, which makes sense, given that graffiti artists face certain pressures that other artists don't have to worry about. What I'm looking for is the technique itself. I watch again the close-ups of his painting arm in action. He holds the can lightly, like a master cellist whose limb simply flows along with the bow. Even though I know that technically he's spraying a concrete wall along a railroad and if the cops caught him he'd be in trouble, he wields those cans with such brio that I want to applaud. It's authentic virtuosity, in which the instrument and the body become an unresisting communication line between the artist and the art. As he paints in black, scarlet, yellow, and white, the lines and peaks and curves and dots emerge, a profusion of random aerodynamic flourishes that have been scaled up and distorted, transferred to a ten-foot wall, blazed with color until they form caricature-words and images, and presented as upsettingly graceful street-glyphs. On the soundtrack, there's no revelation in his vague, casual murmurings. The revelation is in the gestures—their sureness, their unselfconscious ease, the way he casts them across the entire range of his reach. *Whatever-you-wanna-do*.

Ok. So, what do I want to do? I finally decide to draw something—not sure what—with oil-based pastel sticks. This choice is not because I have any talent with them but because their soft, powdery texture is pleasingly at odds with their intense color. My lack of skill is a given, but I accept it and dismiss it so it doesn't interfere with the task at hand. To engage my own imagination, I need the part of my mind that plays and putzes around, even when it's incompetent or badly wounded, or both. I'm seeing my little brother now through the lens of my own grief, but I need that lens defogged, as cleared as possible of sadness to allow me an unobstructed view. I'm waiting: a new idea is going to happen in the present; something brand-new is literally going to occur to me. It doesn't matter if it starts out as a useless scribble—the dreaming mind is awake and about to act. It's a thrill I can't manufacture, because this mind is the one that's not in my control... and it's the one where he is still present.

I fix my attention on the person of my little brother. This means looking outward at pictures of him, looking inward at my memories, and stirring random little bits together to see if they generate any new ideas. It involves studying what's in front of me and thinking about what I know of him, things he liked, and things he did, what he wore, what expressions he used. I'm acutely aware of his death, but I'm also outside it. My two awarenesses debate, and eventually they stop arguing and start working:

*He's gone. No words for this kind of sad. Like in that speech from* Romeo *and* Juliet *that Mrs.Wierman made us memorize in tenth-grade English and that evidently I can have no hope of forgetting, when Romeo says,"sick and pale with grief"—that's exactly right.*

Yes...but right now we're making something. Concentrate.

*But I can't believe I'm sitting here trying to make a picture to commemorate my little brother who's dead.*

I know. Focus on this.

*I shouldn't have to be doing this. It's wrong that I should have to make do with such futile, pathetic comfort.*

That's true. It is wrong. Look at the colors—what fits; what would he like?

*Blue.*

Blue. *There is a blue with a faint green to it, like Caribbean water.*

*He liked paisley.*

*A blue paisley—if it were made of the letters of his own graffiti tag, to represent him—*

—*but stylized differently—it can't be trying to be an imitation—*

*—the letters could form the shape of the paisley—*
*—with other designs inside it, different colors, enclosed—*
*—it looks like a blue teardrop—*
*—a teardrop that contains things...*

The drawing is already becoming something about him, and about me, and about me missing him. Fully aware, I've nevertheless completely forgotten my breathing and the fact that I'm in a Present Moment or indeed any moment at all. And that's when I notice: sorrow will yield to curiosity. While I'm studying what I know of him, I'm out of my own way. It's a precarious perch that I know I won't be able to maintain for very long; like a graffiti artist, I know my time to work here is limited. But the air in this place is so soft that my lungs can breathe without hurting. My mind can do its thing, wield its thought-paints, and I'll be the unresisting communication line while it does whatever it wants to do. This isn't the past, future, or present, but a jumble—and timeless.

* * *

The present moment is often described as if it's a kind of magical, self-sufficient vacuum. But our experience of it is not. The moment of "now" is informed by our experience (what has gone before), and by expectation (what we anticipate will come later). Without mind-altering substances, it seems impossible to escape a Now that's steeped in the pain of lost past and lost future. But there is a way to do it.

What is so mesmerizing about creating? It requires presence of mind, but it's not just passive waiting. It's a willful act, a willingness to invite, knowing something will emerge but not knowing what it is, knowing you'll need to *do* something that you can't foresee yet. Creating something commemorative, a craft or a music mix or some other memorial, isn't only about opening a mental cage and letting go of inhibitions. Nor is it simply a bath in memories. Making something in someone's memory requires you to work with things that are true *even though* your loved person is dead and you're sad and pale and sick. To do this work, you concede those two truths and then, for the moment, dismiss them, because you need all your mental resources free and undistracted, awaiting your creating-self's impulses.

You have to marshal things. Patience to wait for ideas, for one thing. Then, when all the wayward ideas begin to fly out of the opened mental cage, you can't just flail around among them— you have to marshal your self-discipline in order to stick to the task, to keep yourself from getting scattered. The pain of loss keeps wanting to intrude and has to get nudged aside, condensed a little bit, penned up, kept at bay so it's not taking up all your mind-space. The ideas need room to run around loose. Then the hardest part: you have to watch the ideas running around. Harder than the hardest part: you have to feel and sift through your own reactions without censoring, yet without letting your reactions overcome you. Then you marshal the ideas themselves, herd them and sort and re-sort, and bring them into all kinds of random arrangements, until something about what you've got surprises you and begins to take on meaning.

The intense focus turns out to be a startlingly effective shield against those talons of pain that have had you in their clutches all this time. Character study is done from a kind of remove, a drawn-back view in which the lost person's existence is immutable no matter what the conditions are in this instant. It requires a detachment from the loss, a detachment from the moment—the instant and the pain—of now, in order to dwell in a larger sense of what simply is.

## Chapter 37

# Still

(Separation versus Separateness)

*I hear it in the deep heart's core.*
—W. B. Yeats, "The Lake Isle of Innisfree"

Creation gets under way, but there's more. While I think I'm simply remembering his qualities, a bias creeps in—a temptation to dwell on the ways he and I were similar. *He loved blue and so do I. We both had a preference for Mom's heart-shaped oatmeal cookies, and baby animals (or anything vulnerable for that matter), and candy, and wandering away prematurely from the dinner table...*It's comforting to think about the things we shared, as if we two were particularly connected by them, which I guess we were. But in order to see his true self, I have to give equal respect to the ways in which he and I are different. *James Brown, skateboarding, banjo, paintbrushes, curly hair: him. Chopin, the Cocteau Twins, dancing rumba, piano, pencils, straight hair: me.* Why should this feel authentic yet unsettling?

It's the same combination of anxiety and thrill that occurs when I happen upon a National Weather Service website about the layers of the earth's atmosphere. (The topic is something I don't know anything about, but I become interested in it as part of thinking about the thinness of air, and difficulties with breathing, and that sort of thing.) First is the troposphere, closest to the earth; this layer is for clouds and the various events that we call "weather." Further up is the stratosphere, where weather balloons fly, getting literally above it all. Higher still is the mesosphere, where meteors leave their burning trails. Fourth of the five layers is the ironically named thermosphere, which is extremely hot in temperature but so thin, the website explains, that it would feel cold on human skin. Finally there is the exosphere, the highest level up. Furthest from the earth's surface, the exosphere is the place where, according to the website, atoms and molecules escape into space.

It seems a curious word choice, "escape"—as if to be away from the planet were to get free of something. It's amazing but also a concern, to think about those escaping atoms. They're untethered and it's entirely natural that they drift without limitation, but once they separate themselves too much, they might drift impossibly far away, beyond reach. Exactly like my little brother.

I'm tempted to think that our similarities were the tethers preventing him from being lost to me. Cataloguing our differences is authentic but unsettling. To allow him his ultimate differentiation, I'd have to include the final way in which he and I are different: he is dead while I am still alive. I've despised this fact since I first learned it. "I know you're an individual, but this is really taking things too far!" is what I'd say to him, if I could.

However. Even though it feels as if a part of me has died, I remember: He's also (and first) distinct from me and from everyone else. He is a person, complete and entire, unto himself. He has slipped the bonds of human form, but his existence can never be canceled or undone. If I suspend my sense of having lost a part of myself, I can better contemplate him as a unique person who wasn't me, and who still isn't me. Even now, his identity is still intact. I befriend that word, "still"—I take coffee breaks with it, I put a dish of nectar out on my mental porch for it, I

encourage it to visit me as much as it likes, I smile companionably when it does. That word has outlasted his death. "We think
of you as ours, but mysteriously and foremost, you were yours,
and even though you're gone, there's still a 'you,'" I would say
to him, if I could.

This awareness is rare, remote, very stilled…like the mind's
exosphere, a strange and fantastical place with no outer edge, no
safety, and therefore no limits.

\* \* \*

We delight in how our loved one is similar to us. We bask in
the peas-in-a-pod kinship. We remember differences more wist-
fully, because there's not so much camaraderie in them. Besides
highlighting the fact that we were not alike in everything, differences literally keep us apart by defining our individuality and
making us more aware of that unbreakable distance between
ourselves and everyone else——the no-man's-land of loneliness. Difference is the ultimate indicator of why we go on after
someone has died: They've died but we haven't. We're separate.

At first we might panic at this idea, and lash out with a con-
tradiction: *No! I'll never "let go"——they'll always be a part of me!* But
that's not what's going on here. It's worth looking more closely
at what detachment and being separate really mean.

It's not just that they've gone where we can't, for the
moment, follow. Our loved one's distinct self is the thing we
cherish most. It's the thing that can't be recreated or replaced
when someone dies, except by pretending. If we could recapture
it, then there would be no actual loss, and no grief. But we can't
recapture it; it's separate from us.

This separateness is our universal condition, something we paradoxically all share. When we're infants, separation threatens the security of bonding, the safety of togetherness…but separation is not the same thing as separateness. As we grow, there's excitement and a rightness in emerging as a separate self—we don't want to be glued to others; we want to live our own lives, because only then are we free to share. A certain distance lets us be our unique selves and see others as their own unique selves. The distance that separates two beings may be the no-man's-land of loneliness, but it's also the livingplace of love. Maybe the opposite of separation anxiety isn't fusion but separateness appreciation.

The ability to glory in our loved one's otherness invites us to detach from two things:

(1) the person's death
(2) the physical, immediate form of the person themselves.

Both detachments seem terrifying. It takes a certain daring even to attempt them, because always there is the primitive fear: *How can I risk "detaching" in any way, now of all times?* The answer to that frightened question comes to us when we take the risk and do it. It doesn't mean we unclasp some sort of hold we had on them. It means that just as we would adjust a book to a comfortable reading distance or hold a photo at arm's length in order to see the smallest details clearly, we situate ourselves apart from, but close to, our loved one—not so close that we confuse them with their own death, and not so close that we confuse them with ourselves, but just far enough that this person can come into perfect focus.

When we see the difference between aloneness and detachment, we unshackle ourselves from time and from hurt, and the reward is a new awareness of extraordinary clarity and sweetness.

This is the best vantage point for appreciating the other person's inviolate self. We can't possess what's immutable about them—we never could. But from here, we're calmed enough to perceive that it's still there.

For all the privileges we've lost now that they've died, something is unchanged: when we consider them as individuals, we can admire their uniqueness at any time we choose. This is something that can never be lost.

## CHAPTER 38

# The Nature of Connections

(Maintaining Our Regard)

How to achieve this comforting distance, this near-enough-ness? It's all very well to appreciate his individuality, but is there anything that could keep me connected—and in what way—to someone I'll never be able to contact again? Is acknowledging his separateness the only thing I have left? I hate having to struggle along with such inadequate sustenance. I've had this thought a million times, and never seem to get an answer.

I go back to the graffiti video, to the very end, where the screen has gone blank but the sound has been left on, for a kind of last-minute outtake. His voice comments on the limited option of spray paints he'd brought that day. "These are the ugliest fucking colors," his voice says matter-of-factly. *Exactly*, I think. But even though I've watched this video countless times already, this time I notice something that escaped me before: he stated a clear opinion about the color options, but he still painted with them because that's what he had to work with.

I return to my question but ask it slightly differently: Of the things that make up a human relationship, what can I do with what I've got left? I can recognize him (although he's very separate from me in a way I don't like). I am I, and he is he. He's just like me and very unlike me. There's also a wish for exchange, to share aspects of life: ideas and opinions and experiences.

(Preferences; tasks and milestones; memories and newly discovered songs; frights and wishes. Silences and laughs. Amazements.) That part—the exchange—is what's missing. Can that still exist?

I can eat a marshmallow Peep and be aware that I could probably have talked him into putting one (or more) into a cup of cocoa in sheer sugar-loving excess. I can go to a store and see a gawky plush chicken or a coffee-table book about skylines and think, *Good birthday gift for Dave*, although I can never be totally certain because I can't ask him. I have to guess. But I *notice* the coffee-table book, the chicken, bands with irresistible names like "Tame Impala" that I'd feel compelled to ask him if he'd heard of, railroad oil-tankers with pristine sides that seem unfinished without a colorful spray-paint design, and many other things, in a way I wouldn't have done if I hadn't known him.

I struggle for months to make an oil painting based on a freeze-frame from the graffiti video, showing his feet and khaki-clad legs as he's walking the tracks like a transient. I hang the painting where I can see it every day, so it becomes a kind of visual meditation to defuse whatever chaos is happening around me. Maybe that's a form of ongoing exchange. "I'd have bought that CD for you if I'd been your Secret Santa this year, because I know you'd appreciate how cute the idea of a tame impala is," I would say to him, "and I would have played Lessov's 'Ever After' on YouTube for you and said I think it sounds sad even though it's in a major key, and you probably would have said you thought so too, only it would have been with a simple definitive 'Mm-hm' in that inimitable voice of yours. I know you're not here, but you're here in my mind all the time," I would tell him, if I could.

I water a philodendron in a basket that has been given to me as a sympathy gift. The plant survives several moves, and I'm careful to make sure it always has enough water and plant food. Its lustrous heart-shaped leaves frame the photo of Matt and Dave as little kids that I've always kept on display. When Dave was in college, my mom gave him a cutting from one of my overgrowing spider plants, which grew into a full-sized one that he kept. She has now given me back a cutting from it, and I nurture that along too. It thrives.

* * *

What happens after we concede their separateness, and begin more carefully to appreciate—not just with longing, but *actively*—the unchangeable things? A new understanding of connections, the growth of new ones and the fortification of old ones. Initially, we cling to our objects and mementos with a fervor that can border on the defensive, until we begin to understand the larger nature of connection, and understand where it really resides.

What we're trying to do is learn not to undo a bond, but to internalize it more completely than we had to before the death. It takes a long time, even longer if we've never had a good opportunity to internalize any sense of security. How does a little kid learn to stop needing a security blanket or favorite toy, if, after all, it's his talisman against vulnerability? It doesn't matter that the toy can't protect him—it's his mental image of the toy that protects him from fear. When he ventures out into the alien world, the blanket provides a sense of the safety and comfort of home. It's not until later, after the kid's been out there awhile, that he starts to carry safety around with him as something nonphysical. He learns to carry that sense of safety with him in his mind. He can be patient until the next time he takes refuge in a safe haven. The mental image is enough.

It's easy to forget just how little of the physical world we really need, to preserve connections. But it's only after they're safely reinforced, and interesting new ones forged, that we can rest. It's only then that we let go of our anxiety about the words "letting go," because that idea refers only to the physical, and we've already done that because we've had no choice. But the nonphysical? What we let go of is not the lost person but our own desperation. We become students of the longest patience a person ever attempts to practice.

Our part of the connection has *always* been within—our part with us, their part with them. They're gone, and their part is gone with them...but not ours. We carried half of that connection and we're still alive, so it makes sense to try and maintain something of it, just as we maintain the rest of our living self. It's not a fantasy or a psychosis, because it's grounded in reality: we know we'll never see the person again in this existence. Sometimes we like to pretend they're still alive—that is, still in perceivable existence in the world as we know it—even if we know it's a fantasy. We don't have to pretend, though. To be perfectly aware that we're here and they're not here paradoxically keeps the connection *real*. But we also don't know what being dead is. Maybe it's presumptuous to assume we can still relate to someone who has died, but it's just as presumptuous to assume that we *cannot* relate to them.

If we don't know how to relate to someone our five senses can no longer perceive as "here," then how do we nurture a bond that's still alive despite this person's disappearance? Maybe we can endure the rest of our lives without them, by maintaining our regard for them. We revisit our memories and apply what we know to present-day situations—*What would he say about this scenario, what might she say about that situation? I wonder if he can hear me asking questions? Would she love this movie or think it was pointless?*

We can ease back on chasing the answers and instead practice the contemplation itself. When it has become an unthinking habit to do this, whether it's addressing our concept of the person in thought or just wondering what they'd be doing today if they were here, then it becomes natural to need fewer physical things. It becomes natural to relax the literal grip, once we've fortified the mental image of the continued meaning that the person has for us.

Sometimes we don't need any confirmation, we don't need hard evidence, and we don't need our affection mirrored back to us the way it once was. There are facets of ourselves that only exist now, because our loved one existed here too. There are ideas we have that are inspired solely by our memory of them. With no strings attached and no need to cling to or abandon anything, our regard for a person, living or dead, floats within us, sheltered but unconfined. The intangible, when it's strong enough, *is* the essential nature of our connection. The truest attachment we have to our lost loved one can't be severed against our will, because it's made up not just of them, but also of us.

# Lingering Thoughts on Treasure

Our perception of them in the physical world is now out of reach. What's left of our relationship is the part that's longing for renewed exchange. We spend a lot of time with the "wishing" part of loss. We wait alone for what we know we can never have. It's a sad, tiring, endless way to live.

But something is changing. It's a process of turning toward the thing we hate most, which is the irremediable separation. We turn toward it and defy it with the most difficult maneuver: plunging straight into the anxiety and studying it, learning it, understanding it, living with it, and eventually finding what is shining beneath it.

If we don't do this, all we can hope for is numbness, habituation to pain, merely a getting-used-to. However, if we do go back and forth between everyday life and our inner suffering, we will naturally begin to keep living with someone even in the absence of their tangible self.

Two things that allow us to keep from going over the edge are beauty and effort. Memories we may have suppressed seem to regrow like seedlings under a fresh sun, and they become a presence we interact with: we endure them, invite them, and cultivate them. The heart-resonance of our memories is what we've been buffeted by, but it's also what infuses things with so much power. How to encourage a state of resonance, how to seek it out as a means of inspiration? By stirring the depths of memory and creativity on purpose, by wading straight into the bitter in pursuit of the sweet, we enable ourselves to make something that represents the lost person and might have pleased them too.

We can no longer perceive our loved one's presence; we can no longer share with them in the way we're used to. But gone or not, living or dead, doesn't matter; *they are they, and I am I, and we are also a We*.

Finally, it dawns: we can't escape the pain because it's the living love, which is injured but not lost. It's an integral part of who we are, existing within us, solely because of our lost person's own existence. We ourselves become a new kind of presence with whom others interact on a level we haven't known before. Our injured existence now comforts other people who are in pain—and this may be the most exquisite, unlooked-for legacy our beloved has given us.

\* \* \*

No matter what anyone does or
   doesn't do,
There is no such thing as
Life without you.

# The Longing After:
# Ensuing Years

## Chapter 39

# The Banjo in the Other Room

(Being in the Background)

B ack around 2002 Matt made a short video of a train car (a covered hopper) that he and Dave decorated with paint crayons in late autumn—it took them two nights to finish it, and Matt said they were freezing the whole time. (A random commentary on the weather forms part of the graffiti: "brittle cold," it says in a by-the-way scrawl, lest there be any doubt about the conditions under which the artwork was perpetrated.) The video pans slowly, showcasing painted cartoon musicians in a cartoon band, and cartoon dancing figures twirling, grinning, stretching, cavorting in a silent but uninterrupted gambol all across the hopper, so that this otherwise unremarkable train car has become a portable speakeasy, something nocturnal and clandestine that is now also a medley of raucous celebration. It's an *image of music*, music made visible, as if to illustrate that the sound itself is superfluous. Without the sound, your entire visual attention is captured, and you can hear something that isn't actually there.

The video cuts then, to random footage—now it's my parents, talking in their kitchen. Matt, behind the camera, jokingly reminds my mother, "You are being watched, Mom." She smiles distractedly and gives a casual wave as she talks to my dad, who has apparently misplaced something and is rooting around the kitchen in search of it. But their conversation is irrelevant; the riveting thing now, when we watch the video after 2004, is what's audible in the background. Offscreen and soft but very clear, is the sound of Dave playing his banjo around the corner in the next room. Like our dad (a piano virtuoso) and like me (a piano novice), Dave tended to play his banjo in a behind-the-scenes manner, for personal enjoyment rather than for an audience. My mother and I sometimes used to tiptoe to the edge of the family-room doorway to listen; I would gaze dumbfounded at her, and she would whisper, "I *know*!" in acknowledgment of the ludicrousness of how well he played. Sometimes we'd hear the disjointed plucking of strings as he taught himself a new tune, and other times it was the contented strumming of a song he'd mastered and was playing around with. In the video, it's the contented strumming, a rollicking sound so quintessential that the image of the banjo-player himself is superfluous. When all you have is that sound, your entire listening attention is drawn to it—and you can see someone who isn't actually there.

I think of these things many times, now. Can the image of him in the next room—like those greeting cards that promise "He is just away"—hearten me to keep living? I think about past evenings. Specifically, I remember dinner.

Family dinners, when Tim, Mike, and I were young adults visiting, and Matt and Dave were teenagers: the two youngest brothers didn't care so much then about "spending time" with us older siblings, because we didn't have much in common at that point in our various lives. As soon as Matt and Dave finished their meals, they'd go careening out the door with their friends, often amidst our mother's protests: "But your brothers and sister are here! You hardly ever see them and now they're here, and you're racing off with your friends!"

I used to laugh to myself about this. What's the philosophy behind being glad that family members are there, and then walking out the door to be with friends? Were we, as the "abandoned" family members, insulted? Not in the least. There is a sense of security in knowing that for the moment, familiar and friendly people are in the immediate background, so that one is paradoxically comfortable enough to ignore them for a while. As if God's in his heaven, all's right with the world—so you can go hang out with your friends because that's what teenagers really want to do anyway. But it matters that family people are still available somewhere. Matt might not have particularly wanted to talk to us right that minute, but it was nice for him to know that he could when he wanted to; he knew we were around. Dave could get up and slip out the door to be with his friends, because we'd continue to be there even if he left, and it was enough for him just to know that we were there in the background.

It will have to be enough for me, now. I don't want my lost brother's name to become synonymous with sadness, or a signal for a mood to darken, something for others to avoid like an emotional plague, a reminder of sickening pain. So I accept the form he exists in now, which is a form I can't perceive. And if I'm to keep him real, I keep the full round of feeling about his human self.

This means that sometimes he'll be absent, even unthought of, sometimes present and singled out, and sometimes an accidental or a deliberate inspiration, just as if he were here. And often he'll be simply in the background, like the banjo in the other room, or like Tim and Mike and me at a family dinner. In this way, the idea of him will continue to come along, as it ought to have, all along. And his name will continue to represent what it once did: all of the real him, knowable and unknowable alike.

* * *

To feel good, to laugh, to be excited about plans, to do things that have to do with the lost person and things that don't...at first, the very idea of "things that don't have to do with them" is an outrage. It takes a long time to learn that doing things that don't overtly include the lost person doesn't mean we exclude them. In fact, this is how we'd live with them if they were still here. It's not blasphemous or disloyal to sometimes not be thinking of them— on the contrary, it's the ultimate defiance of death, because it's what we do in life.

It's a little like acknowledging that they must always be in the next room. Sometimes this way of looking at our situation will be unwanted, rejected, even despised, because underneath it all is the horrible truth: we can't go talk to them in the literal next room. But the signs of their existence are infinitely better than nothing.

When a little child asks for a piece of cake that is gone, and instead is offered the last few crumbs, at first the child rejects the crumbs. Crumbs are not what he wants; he has stated clearly that he wants a piece of cake. You say that the cake is gone but these are from the cake, and you offer the crumbs again. Rejection, tears, fury: "No! Not crumbs! Don't want crumbs, I want cake!" The crumbs go flying to the ground. OK, fine, it's crumbs or nothing, so it's nothing...you sweep up the crumbs and head for the trash bag, and what happens? Abject panic. Screams: "*Yes I do want the crumbs, give them to me! Iwantthecrumbs I-want-them-I-want-them-I-want-the-crumbs!*" And the crumbs are snatched greedily, guarded protectively. In an instant, a few crumbs have become priceless.

It is a hard lesson to learn, but the switch in perspective is something we've been able to do from a very early age. We'll take what we can get, even if the tears of despair and deprivation are still flowing. We hate having only crumbs available. Even so, we love the crumbs because they are, at least, something we can have, and after all, they are a tiny part of the cake. It's a complicated parcel of feelings to carry around, yet we do it.

## CHAPTER 40

# An Unexpected Ghost

(Shifts in Thought)

When I paint the picture of him walking the tracks, my mother texts me the suggestion that I sign the back of the canvas. I stand in front of it wondering what sort of pen would be best. Without thinking, I start texting back to her: "We should ask Dave." The moment is only a moment; before I finish the first word, "We," I've remembered, and I stop. But instead of despair, there is a piercing delight. Although I'm very familiar with the thought *He's dead,* as of today that fact can no longer always hog the front of the thought-line. Other ideas can get there first again, ideas like *Dave paints; he'll know what kind of pen to use.*

It's a fancy way of saying that for an instant, I forgot that he's gone. Probably it's just the mild confusion of eras in one's own life, the tumble-dry overlapping of memories that seems inevitable once we're out of childhood. But even if it's just a mental glitch, it's also very much like catching a glimpse of my own ghost, someone un-bereft who lives where *he* is still living. Whatever it is, it means this: there will be moments when his death won't have to be automatically the first thing I think of, when I think of him.

\* \* \*

A gently sweet day comes when, even just for a second, we forget that we've lost them. Although impossible to summon at will (much like other people), the self that lived back then is apparently still around somewhere in our head; for that self, the person we've come to think of as "lost" isn't lost at all.

## CHAPTER 41

# Certain Lovely Nights

### (The Permanence of Pain)

Up to now, April has always meant springtime in earnest, with trees frilly as parasols and the daylight beginning to linger after dinner, and the birds, oh the little birds…! But now, beautiful April means something else as well, like the first sweet notes of a threnody. April is the impendingness of May.

May in Pennsylvania is green days unfurling like fronds and soft evenings basking in their own perfume. It's pure coincidence that in this month, my little brother was born, and in it, he died. There are certain lovely nights when the weather is just right, that I see it all clearly, as if it is a new realization. The idea of him lying there beneath the embryonic starlight of May—how desperately this one single thing hurts. If a viper had slithered into my blood, found its way to my heart, and without warning sunk its fangs into the innermost lining, that might feel like this same breath-seizing suddenness, the shock that illogically happens at random moments, years after the fact: *Killed. Alone, crushed, on the ground. My little brother, mine.* I forget everything I've learned about detachment, and the tide of despair rushes in: *This can't still be true. But it is. And how can I endure evenings this beautiful? How can I save my Little Shnookins? Why can't somebody save him?*

On certain lovely nights when the weather is mild and the birds are chirping, I'm unadmirable. I don't want to be glad that things weren't worse. I don't want to be ennobled and have enhanced compassion. I just want him to be living.

I don't want to have New Wisdom Earned Through Great Sorrow. I was a kind person before this; why wasn't that enough? I'd rather be clear, untroubled, whole, with him still here and me naive of this loss. Mike has told me that now he can't stand to listen to a certain song called "My Immortal" by a group called Evanescence; I find it and listen to it and never mention it to him because I understand perfectly and there's no need to discuss it.

Of course I get it: loss is a part of living. But not *this* loss. "Living" was never meant to include such wrongness. My little brother wasn't meant to die so young, in a car crash, without warning. He was meant to live to old age, go to the funerals of the rest of us, burn candles in our memory (or maybe spray paint furtive memorials for each of us, as he'd done on September 11 for the Twin Towers). He was meant to live out his own happy life and eventually die in his sleep after taking peaceful leave of everyone who cared for him. For as long as I'm aware of how things are meant to have happened, then no peace can be made with the unnaturalness of what really happened. It will never be OK.

Every year on April 30, very late at night, I go outside. Sometimes I'll drive to the crash site, and other times I won't, but always I'll be outside in the quiet starlit dark, as May comes into being and (within me) a light goes out.

* * *

Certain days and nights of resurgent protest are in their own way indispensable. They're tantrums sometimes, against the way things are, but mostly they're reminders. The self taken unawares on that single terrible day can't be crushed out completely, and it's on these certain lovely nights that we can feel its labored breathing. And, oddly, feel its strength.

## Chapter 42

# Up the Bank

(Wonder)

*There are more things in heaven and earth...than are dreamt of in your philosophy.*

—William Shakespeare, *Hamlet*

Two years after the trial, the family goes to Wilkes-Barre to celebrate our grandmother's birthday. It's a fun and noisy chaos as large family dinners tend to be, but there's that freight-train line running almost through our grandparents' backyard, and from long experience Tim and Matt can sense the approach of a train even when it's still miles away, even through the ruckus of dinner. In such circumstances, interested parties stop whatever they're doing, dash outside, and ascend the railroad bank to watch the train, even if it means abandoning a plate of half-eaten food. The extended family here is highly familiar with this behavior and accepts it as a matter of course, and this time is no different; it's the middle of dinner, but Matt, Tim, and our cousin Dan are already preparing to go outdoors. I seldom get to Wilkes-Barre anymore, so I'm excited to go too.

Utterly unlike passenger trains that fly and stop in fitful intervals, a freight train is indifferent to the fussy world of commuters. It doesn't merely interrupt traffic—the authentic thrill of a freight train is that while it lasts, it commands the air and the earth. This evening, the commanded air is already vibrating in the March dusk. We jog down the street and scramble up the bank, guided by the urgency in the initial vague hum as it becomes a steadily deepening rumble. At the top of the bank we emerge from the underbrush and look along the tracks toward the river. There on the trestle bridge, beaming from Kingston on the other side of the river, is the iconic single head-light of the engine. That erratic, brightening eye has immedi-ately fixed us in its impassive gaze. There is no time left; the train is coming.

As it reaches the near side of the river and emerges from the trestle, the pulsing of the engine surges through the ground. The entire railroad bank trembles. You couldn't run even if you wanted to—to see the oncoming trainlight and feel your own heartbeat overtaken by the bottomless bass roar of the engine is to be completely mesmerized. But we haven't come here in order to run away. To hide from the fearsome power would be to miss the passing god.

In a few more seconds the massive engine catches up with its own light and looms up before our eyes, and we're right there waiting for it. The engineers acknowledge us with a blast of the horn, and as always I try to cover my ears and wave at the same time. The engine hurtles past, and now the process of Watching the Train begins. The boxcars are coursing briskly in an endless clack-clack of wheels, with twilight flashing between them. Their sidings are plastered with graffiti, and despite the nearly impossible chances of seeing a car with any of Dave's on it, I find myself trying to study the train cars one by one, a troublesome task when I'm only a few feet from their towering height and speed. For long minutes, we're hypnotized by the film-reel blur of train-sky-train-sky-train. At last the end of the train is approaching, when suddenly I see it: a dull-ochre boxcar with the letters ARSON painted on it in silvery-white——our little brother's graffiti tag. I point and shout but it's going so fast that it's already gone.

The remaining cars pass and then we're left behind in the sudden spiraling nothingness that is the train's wake. We watch the last car receding, and already I miss the trainlight and what it signifies: the lonely, the long-drawn, and the legacy of telescoping vertigo, the trick of the eye that feels like you yourself are moving when you stare at the empty air. We loiter in the dusk, still watching, when something unexpected occurs. Inexplicably, the train appears to be losing speed...is it slowing down?...it *is* slowing down. With a long desultory clanking, and the groan and screech of laboring brakes, it ponders to a halt.

The train has stopped, the last car only a few hundred yards away from us. Tim and Matt say this happens sometimes, when the engineers stop at a Burger King a few miles up——nothing inexplicable about that. But we don't linger to discuss it; we set off at a sprint toward those last few cars. It's unpleasant to run so soon after eating, and my ankles twist a couple times on the uneven stones. I run faster.

Quickly we reach the last car and now it's we who barrel alongside the waiting train. Scanning each car as we run, we soon find the one we're looking for. We gather breathlessly before it like pilgrims at a newly unveiled Rembrandt, and Matt confirms that the graffiti tag, dated 2002, is indeed our brother's handiwork. Matt calls our parents on his cell phone; I haven't seen my dad up here in many years, and my mother never, but after a few minutes they both come scrabbling up the railroad bank along with some other relatives, including our uncle Lee, who brings a camera.

With each flash, the silver lettering gleams into the dusk. We take turns posing next to it. We look and look, murmuring quietly, stepping up close to touch the paint, standing back to take it all in. The train stands patiently, like a beast of burden temporarily out to pasture, until presently a hiss of air heralds its readiness to depart. It stirs and glides into motion, and the boxcar trundles gently away from us into the night.

We watch it go. No one debates what the boxcar "means." For this moment, we're in its thrall, basking in its authenticity. Underneath the marvel is a quietness, a cessation, something with mercy in it. If those dying of thirst were each given a cup of water, this is the hush that would fall as they drank.

* * *

At first it's just a sense, a sensation—our attention is caught. We stop what we're doing, uncertain. Disbelief tries to shove us back. Finally, hesitant but real: wonder.

Is it a "sign"? Is there a possibility, could this be some kind of communication? Some of us are certain; others of us aren't. People tend to prefer decisive answers; we want certainty. We'd like to have this situation confirmed as a sign from someone dead who can still try to communicate with us, or we want it catalogued as merely a coincidence or possibly a stress-induced hallucination; in any case, we want it explained. The option we often forget is to cease trying to categorize. We can decide to undecide.

It isn't easy. But it used to be. Back in our own beginning, wondering was our first approach to the world. When we're very young, wondering is like breathing; we do it naturally, and no one faults us for asking questions, or for not being able to figure things out on our own. We're smiled at for our naïveté, and we're given as many answers as possible, and gradually we learn how to search out the answers for ourselves. We learn how to Do-the-Homework. Investigate, experiment, inquire, do some background reading, ask an expert, look it up online, do our own research. When we finally reach the limits of our knowledge, our imagination, or our resources, we say: "I don't know."

We don't particularly like having to say that. Besides earning us the disappointment of authority figures (such as teachers or supervisors), and maybe the ridicule of others (like classmates or colleagues), admitting we don't know shows us our own limits. But it's an opportunity to re-engage the state of mind that deals in possibilities. It's a state of mind we gradually outgrow as we become more skilled at finding the answers and more frustrated or ashamed when we can't answer. And because our adult lives require us to comprehend a great many things, pure wonder becomes a luxury of sorts, this taking time simply to marvel at something without the pressure to figure it out and explain it.

*I don't know.* What we do know is that our limitations exist, but we don't know where those limitations are, and experience suggests that there's probably something beyond them. Humankind has already discovered that plenty exists beyond our ability to detect. We've got all sorts of machines, microscopes, telescopes, microphones, seismographs, and our own imaginations to peer past the limits of our unaided senses, to find the things around us that are too small or too big to register on our bodily detection systems. Hamlet, Shakespeare's most famous ponderer, issues a telling message to any suffering human: "There are more things in heaven and earth...than are dreamt of in your philosophy." There is more to existence than whatever our particular brains can conceive of. It's when we confront this that we perceive the imperceptible; it's then that we turn our gaze on that which can't be seen.

When we've lost someone, our desperation goes quiet during those moments of pure and vivid wondering. Maybe there's nothing. Maybe there's something. In terms of knowing, that's as far as we can go before we branch away into issues of religion, faiths, beliefs. But wondering has no limits.

We're forced to transcend matter and certainty, to look beyond the things we usually trust. A mystery can be turned over in the mind indefinitely and never be solved. We can suspect, we can fear, we can hope, we can think we know, and we can fervently believe or just as fervently discount, but always there will be not knowing for sure.

Then how can we tolerate more than one possibility without ever knowing certain answers for sure? We can do what we did when we were very young—look, take different perspectives, consider from various angles. We can figure that one day, we'll find out for ourselves, but we don't know when that day might be.

Between despair and certainty, wonder sits right in the middle. Like the exact physical center-point of a line—you can trace the line and know that you've touched that point, but you'll never know for certain exactly where it is. Wonder is where the truth hides.

## CHAPTER 43

# A Sandcastle

(What Strengthens With Time)

Though it's irrational, every now and then I have a sense that since May 1, 2004, nothing, not time or history, is quite real anymore. His death, the story of it and my life since I learned of it, are somehow apocryphal. A myth.

As if by unspoken agreement, the four remaining siblings seem to have privatized the loss, put it away for safekeeping in some durable mental vessel that can be carried for many years—theoretically, I suppose, far longer than our parents will have to carry it, although there's no guarantee of that. Over time, our little brother's lack of voice, the silence and the absence, have become their own inviolate monument. To avoid the topic of his death is not to behave as if he never existed, and it's not that his death itself is denied. Instead, our silence on the matter means that his death is denied *sovereignty*. It doesn't deserve to cast a shadow over everything else about him. It doesn't deserve to be announced with trumpets before anyone makes a random comment related to him, nor does the mention of his name trail off in violins afterward. He deserves to be someone besides our-brother-who-died. Our refusal to couch everything in terms of his absence has become our way of resettling him into his rightful place in our mini-universe. Why must that one fact (the fact of his death) override everything else? Maybe this is the ultimate denial, the denial that allows us to feel happy talking about him instead of always focused on the terrible truth of his absence. But there is no mistake: although no comment is made on it, the awareness of his absence gains strength with each passing day.

Nearly seven years after the fact, I'm in a car with a friend; we're listening to a random mix of music. It's James Blunt singing "Stay the Night," and The Cure singing "Friday I'm In Love," and then Annie Lennox comes on, singing "Into the West"—which instantaneously brings me back to a phone conversation with Mike in the days before Dave's funeral. I look out the window and blink, and then I succumb without fanfare, as gently as a sandcastle in a single wave. I ask my friend, can he please play something else? He's startled.

"Bad associations?" he asks.

"Sad ones," I say, "from when we were memorializing my little brother." I explain no further and I'm quiet for a long time.

This particular song has triggered a different kind of remembering. I'm being struck by all the days of my little brother's life, how it wouldn't take very long to count them one by one. I'm struck by how long it's been since I've seen him and by the fact that I've learned to wait indefinitely. When did I learn to wait? Wait for what? It's not that I'm consciously expecting him to return, but always some part of me sits in vigil, always simply aware that I'll have to live out my whole life before I can stop waiting. This ability to wait gets stronger, its roots growing deeper every year, like an oak tree. And I'm struck by the freshness of one wish that flowers continually like a living vine around the oak of patience: *I want my little brother back*. Sometimes I wonder: Will the vine choke the tree? Or will the tree support the vine no matter how heavily it hangs? Can anyone ever explain how a person goes on living when someone indispensable has died?

I find something, not an answer but an echo of the question, in a song called "Pain Lies on the Riverside," by a group called Live. It's not so much in the lyrics, although they're apt enough, but in the way a clamor rises around the melody, and in the vicious, fangs-bared anguish of the lead singer's voice, which moves with the music but fights with it too, as if he's being hacked apart from the inside but *will* sing anyway, all of it, to the last drawn-out sigh. I listen to the song while I'm driving at night, and its agonized power comforts me. When May comes around again and I sit in my car at the crash site at one in the morning looking at the stars, it's comforting to think that that light was shining in the same time span in which my little brother was living here.

One day I write a tiny story that I hope he might have liked, a little silly thing about creatures and light crossing multiple worlds, light crossing time, light *defining* time. As I work on it I wonder how he would have illustrated it if I'd asked him to. I wonder about all the things he could have done with it, and all he might ever have done, and how all of life is diminished without his presence, and how I wish we could have known him just a little bit longer.

### The Forelighting of Today

*A fish swam among the reeds, in and around and between and among the grasses of rainbow-green. When sunlight shimmered down, the fish could hardly see for all the brightness, and the grasses were enough. But on cloudy days or soft dim night, the fish could see up, up, up, through the water to the flowers above, in that alien world outside the water. Flowers in colors like sky and lemon and berry-pink, with soft blue-opal stems. And best of all, on clear nights the little fish could see the stars and even a glimpse of light pinging from the planets, frosting the moon, and shining all the way down to tiny fish in unknown ponds, fish who*

*maybe don't know that what they're seeing is the light of yesterday, light
that's a few minutes old already, the light of the tomorrow that's coming;
fish who maybe do not understand that somewhere else, that same light
is already called Today.*

\* \* \*

It's always been remarked upon, the things that can happen "in the blink of an eye." People say it about kids growing up, but someone being born and growing up and dying, and being missed every day afterward, can happen in the blink of an eye, too. The immediacy of the pain of loss may be hidden for days, weeks, years, but can surge in full force, without a moment's notice, in the time it takes to look away and blink. A flash-flood of grief can take us down like a sandcastle.

"Accepting the death" is only half of what happens. People want the process to mean this: acknowledge the death and take time to heal, and begin again to enjoy life, with appropriate memories but without permanent repercussions. But we can't accept a blow that powerful and emerge unscathed. Acknowledgment of the truth, the taking-in of reality, is necessary, but it damages us. What makes the damage ultimately bearable is that it's consciously accepted, along with the facts. In the moment we acknowledge that our loved one is dead, we also accept a lifetime of pain about it. A person may be lost, but the love for them is not. It will always yearn for the one it belongs to.

A bereaved boy is not some poor thing trying to be happy but lost somewhere inside the shell of a crying boy; he *is* the crying boy. A grieving woman has not disappeared into an altered personality of a depressed woman; she *is* a depressed woman. Of course they aren't only those things, but they are partly those things. Sadness and anguish become a permanent part of the bereaved person's full self. Not their whole being but a part of it, and this part will come to the fore at times, during all the years that follow.

Contrary to appearances, we've been sensitized, not deconditioned. It hurts more, not less. Some days we accept, other days merely acknowledge, and still other days numbly observe, the weaving of this abiding grief into our own life. Time provides an opportunity to gain strength, but it seems to give strength to everything indiscriminately. So what really happens to us, over time?

Over time, we figure out for ourselves how to shift the burden of pain to different angles on our shoulders, how to lean on things such as our memories, or sympathetic friends and strangers, loyal pets, or the simple physical support of a dirt pile we once played in with a sense of comfort in its solidity. We find support when our patience alone isn't sufficiently strong to sustain us. Just as in weightlifting, our strength comes only with the repeated efforts we make—even just the effort to get up each morning when it seems futile, to go through another day when we're only half-attentive, meet another evening and another dawn, and another, and another. We make a practice of it, but never a perfection.

The ability to compartmentalize, to control our emotions in public—that ability gets stronger, too. We're more adept at keeping ourselves focused on today, or at least giving the impression that we're focused on today. We get more skillful at stopping our thoughts before they become too clear, if we happen to be in a situation where we want to maintain our equilibrium.

And what of our ability to simply miss the absent one? As our patience grows in strength, so does the wish to have our loved person back. A thousand times, and a thousand more times after that: *I wish you were still here—all of the real you, knowable and unknowable alike.* The intensity of this wish grows astonishingly stronger with the passing of time. At times, even years later, the loss is a brand-new hurt that can't be deconstructed, soothed into silence, bandaged gently, or folded away in lavender. Memories and dreams, objects and ceremonies—none of these will ever be a substitute for the real, living person. What happens to us over time is just this: we live paradoxically; we live with without-ness.

No one expects an oceantide to find a happy medium and stay there; by its nature it rises and ebbs and rises and ebbs, without end. It's just how it is.

## CHAPTER 44

# A Clay Castle

### (The Massive Importance of Minutiae)

Thanksgiving 2012 is our ninth without him. While we're cleaning up after dinner, my mother explains that the other day, she was in the downstairs bathroom and accidentally knocked a little clay castle Dave had made in fifth grade off the windowsill. "It shattered," she says ruefully. She was deeply distressed; she'd cleaned that bathroom a million times in the past and never disturbed the castle; she couldn't imagine how this happened. She'd gathered up the pieces but she could only find three of the four turrets. She'd looked and looked for the fourth one but couldn't find it in that tiny bathroom. She'd gone upstairs and cried. She guessed it was because she'd been reading the information from the trial earlier, the descriptions of the crash scene—

I immediately abandon my plans to get home in a timely fashion. "Where are the pieces?" I ask. "Maybe it can be glued back together." She brings the broken bits of clay to the kitchen. I put on an apron, sit at the kitchen counter, and assess the damage: a few big chunks, a dismaying number of tiny fragments. We put down paper towels and gather tweezers, toothpicks, and different types of glue. We lay out the fragments and then begin piecing them together like a puzzle, conferring about which connects to which, trying different combinations this way and that. Based on the evidence of raw edges and finished edges, we surmise that there were only three turrets; there's no lost fourth turret because Dave must not have included one in the original design of this castle. I speculate that maybe he'd intended it to be a ruin, given how ruins fascinate in a way that brand-new buildings don't. (Various other family members meander to and fro in the background, but no one disturbs the murmuring progress of our work. None of us knows that the fourth turret will turn up under a radiator, three years later.)

When we finally know what goes where, it's time for the tweezers and toothpicks and glue that are arrayed before us like surgical instruments. We reconstruct the broken castle, one wall at a time, fleck by ridiculously small fleck, grey to grey, green to green, blue to blue, white to white. It takes a couple hours and some good-natured struggling with the tiny ladder that won't stay propped in place and falls repeatedly when I try to bolster it. But at last the castle is reassembled. The broken seams hardly show at all. We're inordinately pleased.

Thanksgiving.

\* \* \*

Little things, sometimes the most insignificant trifles that no one else would look twice at, carry so much weight that it's no wonder they sometimes shatter and have to be repaired.

# Chapter 45

# Saudade

"Saudade" is a song. It's actually the title of many different songs, but the one I know is by a group called Love and Rockets. It was on a mix Tim made for me back when we were college students, and now in 2012 I randomly search it out on YouTube. The music can't be described—is it contented or restless, sweet or sad, lovely or lost, spiraling into the distance or paused and hovering somewhere? It echoes within itself, the tones waking and dissolving like dream-remnants but with a recognizable melody buoying all of it, carrying it along and away. To hear it is to be suspended, instantaneously and completely, in a wistful state of being whose beauty has no words in it at all.

Fittingly, the song is an instrumental, relying only on its title to suggest what inspired the music. It's never occurred to me until now to find out what the title means. I look it up on Wikipedia—it turns out to be a Portuguese word that apparently has no English translation and doesn't lend itself to easy definition. As I read various interpretations, I'm awed and silenced:

*A sort of painful nostalgia, a deep and wistful state of longing for something or someone that one was fond of and which is lost; with repressed knowledge that the object of longing will never return.*

*The love that stays after someone is gone.*

237

*An incompleteness one unconsciously wants to never completely resolve.*

*An emptiness, like someone who should be there in a particular moment is missing and the individual feels this absence.*

*"I miss you," but with a much stronger tone.*

Reading this reminds me of another of my favorite words, *ineffable*, which means "indescribable or inexpressible." Too extremely anything to be explained. There's a lot to these words—they each put into a word, that which can't be put into words. They offer themselves as, admittedly and by definition, a totally inadequate substitute. They're words that let you use them for life's extremes, when there's nothing you can hope to say. With simplicity, they acknowledge how much is beyond them. They're words that don't speak; mute words that stand as guardians of things impossible to express.

As usually happens when I start out looking for one thing online and end up lost, flitting deeper and deeper into links and cross-references, my initial search has led me into all manner of pages and articles. I come back finally to the Wikipedia site and scroll all the way to the bottom of the page, where there are lists of references and suggested links to related terms that the reader who originally looked up "saudade" might find relevant or interesting. My gaze alights: there on the "See Also" list is the Japanese phrase *Mono no aware*—the same phrase on the cover of Dave's photo album, which he'd translated on the back: *beauty of the impermanent*. At this, I smile through the brightest possible tears as I miss my little brother—it's a wistful state of being whose beauty has no words in it at all.

* * *

Beauty + impermanence = saudade.

# Lingering Thoughts on the Longing After

T he first years after loss are only the beginning.

It takes a very long time for the death even to begin to relinquish its reign in our mental spotlight.

Some long, later time in the future that we can't grasp, we'll begin the process of extricating our loved one from their own death. Imperceptibly, we approach a new ability: the ability to consider the death as part of their life, but not the only part, or even the most important part.

The ability to do this doesn't come until we've had a lot of practice shifting our perspective, thinking about all the things we know about the person's life—the end of it, the middle, the beginning, and the unforeseeable effects that single life will have in the future.

We know saudade if we ever lose anyone we love. We may seem to stop waiting and stop hoping, but we never stop wishing. We may not die of this longing, but we'll surely die with it.

Even so, deliberate appreciation of our loved one, and the inspiration of their personality, help to lessen our railing against the universal transience of this life and the transience of each of us within it.

Awareness of that transience is our lot, but so is the ability to discern and cherish, within a life that was too fleeting, the ineffable Always.

CPSIA information can be obtained
at www.ICGtesting.com
Printed in the USA
LVOW08s1913280417
532511LV00048B/213/P